Further Along the Lines...

More writings from Ross-shire

Ross-shire Writers

Published by:
Ross-shire Writers
41 Urquhart Road
Dingwall
IV15 9PE

Printed by Dingwall Printers

Cover Photo: © David Ian Stewart

ISBN 978-0-9554876-1-3

Commendations for *Along the Lines* . . .

It's vibrant. An impressive collection of poems and prose which capture the essential qualities of style, technique and tone. Congratulations.

Comments from David St John Thomas
at Charitable Trust prize giving.

This anthology is a treasure chest. Everything it contains is a surprise. It is thought-provoking, interesting and reader-friendly. It would make an ideal gift as it contains something to appeal to everyone.

Isabelle Morgan in her feature on Book of the Week
in the Press and Journal (2007)

ACKNOWLEDGMENTS

Ross-shire Writers wishes to acknowledge the contribution of a number of people in the production of this anthology.

The Editorial Board has had the arduous task of selecting, editing, cajoling and finally compiling the stories and poems that follow.

David Stewart, keen photographer and husband of one of our members, has provided the cover photograph.

Peter Smith LL.B, barrister, has cast his legal eye over all the contributions.

Dingwall Printers has printed the book and assisted us in the layout and format.

Our thanks go to them all.

CONTENTS

FOREWORD

"Further Along the Lines . . ." is the third anthology produced by Ross-shire Writers and the second to be published. This follows the highly successful *"Along the Lines . . ."* which was launched in 2007 as part of the Highland Year of Culture.

In the Writer's Circle Anthology section of the prestigious David St. John Thomas Charitable Trust competition, *"Along the Lines . . ."* won first place, being awarded the Writers' News trophy. The competition is held nationwide in the United Kingdom and this was only the second time that a Scottish Group had won this coveted prize.

Ross-shire Writers is a group which meets regularly. It draws its membership from a wide range of backgrounds, ensuring that the writing is challenging and reflecting a wide range of interests. The group is dynamic and several members and former members have been published in other forums and indeed an ex member won this year's Neil Gunn competition.

We hope you will enjoy the selection of new stories and poems that follow.

ON THOSE DAYS OF CRYSTAL CLEAR
Christina Macdonald

On those days of crystal clear,
Senses heightened,
I can hear and see the beauty of the day.
The thrush's song, the blackbird's trill
The pictures of a sad world's ill
Flee before the morning thrill
Of gardens wet with morning dew,
Tall spires of flowers in deepest blue.
My heart can soar beyond Earth's thrall
And I rejoice again in all
That Nature gives us to enjoy.

On those days of crystal clear
The eye sees brightly, no cloud here
To blind one's vision. Without fear
The eye can feast on vistas, far and near.
The touch of leaf and flower expands
The feel of Nature in our hands
The softness of the furry leaf
The feather-feel of waving grass
Faint brush on cheek of winds that pass.
The taste of strawberries on the plate
A drift of thyme beside the gate
The spice of pink scents all around
In evening when the sun slips down.

On those days of crystal clear
All senses blend and flow and flower
With every second, every hour
What bliss to have such days as these
When all of Nature seems to please
All our senses and our mind
What better way one's Life to find?

CRUSHED
Louise James

Helen cursed as she sprinted to the bus-stop, arriving just as the No. 25 pulled away. She wasn't going to wait a whole hour for the next one so began the long walk home, down the High Street and into the narrow country road leading to Frinton. She'd done the walk many times since starting work in town and as often as not someone heading to the village would pull over and offer her a lift. Caution about strangers seemed out of place in this part of the county where if you didn't know someone personally you almost certainly knew them by sight. So she was surprised when the black Porsche 911 Carrera pulled up and saw that it wasn't Jake Grant at the wheel. His personalised plates made him easily recognisable as he whizzed around the country lanes, mostly a good twenty miles over the limit. So, no doubt it was his car alright but who was this woman at the wheel? Older than her mother but not as old as Nan. Long frizzy hair, streaked with grey, sticking out untidily from a lime green beret and clashing wildly with the geometric blocks of colour on her jacket. Her round-framed glasses were bright pink, a close match Helen noticed, for her fingerless leather driving gloves.

"Hop in, kiddo!" she smiled, waving expansively at the passenger seat. Her accent was trans-Atlantic, her expression friendly and open. "I'll drop you at the top of the Green if you like." Something in her manner implied that they were old friends and Helen felt somewhat mesmerised as she slid into the plush leather and fastened her seat belt.

"Are you a relation of the Grants?" Helen asked, emboldened by the woman's breezy cheerfulness.

"A relation . . . yes, yes, I am. The Grants' long lost aunt come by for a visit." She laughed, and stretched her right arm across her body to shake Helen's, who had to twist awkwardly to accept her hand. "I'm Theresa. Theresa Grant," she added with a giggle, then pulled her hand back quickly to grab the wheel and manoeuvre nearer the hedge. A rather large van was approaching; Helen recognised Alan from the builder's yard and saw his surprise as he took in the car, its driver and

12

its passenger. Something about the situation made Helen laugh delightedly out loud. No way would she have ever dreamt that she'd be riding in Jake Grant's Porsche, not in a million years. He lived in the Victorian pile on the edge of Frinton where his parents played at arable farming but really made their money from horses and Mr Grant was Master of the Middledale Hunt. And here she was, daughter of the publican at the Bay Tree Inn, speeding through the back lanes in his car. With an aunt that Helen was sure would cause a stir amongst the county set the Grants hung out with.

Helen's good humour at the situation obviously pleased Theresa who joined in the laughter, releasing the wheel and slapping it twice with both hands, a momentary lapse that meant she had to overcorrect on the next bend. Helen was impressed with her quick recovery, and settled back comfortably while they sped on, amazed at the sense of elation that swept over her. Just half an hour ago she was closing up shop at her boring insurance office job, and now! She felt like she never wanted to go back. Wouldn't that stuffed shirt Martin Hardwick die if he could see her now. He'd probably want to check that the mysterious Theresa Grant was insured to drive Jake's Porsche. What a spoilsport he was, always looking for ways to deflate you whenever you were in danger of enjoying yourself. Just yesterday, for example, she suggested that they do up some window boxes for the front of the office. She would have done all the work, and brought in plants her mum had left over, but no, they'd 'only be vandalised' or, 'you'd forget to water them' or something. She sighed in recollection of how dreary she found the work, and wished she could pursue her dream of going to art college in Newcastle. Theresa seemed fine-tuned to Helen's mood, for, just at that moment, she said, "Well, it's Friday and you must be glad you're done for the week. If you aren't in a big rush why don't we swing round to the Malt Shovel in Middledale. Get those cobwebs swept away!" Anticipating a 'yes' before Helen actually opened her mouth, she spun right at the crossroads where the sign indicated eleven miles to the county town. And of course Helen was in total agreement with the scheme. She'd promised to help in the bar at home but it didn't get busy till after eight so there was no hurry.

And she was starving; the Malt did fabulous bar food.

What a great meal they had! Somehow it seemed natural – almost inevitable – that Helen poured out all her unhappiness and frustration: the dead-end job, the dead-wood boyfriend, and the dead-dull village that she seemed unable to escape. Theresa listened attentively, saying little till Helen had finished.

"Well, kiddo," she exclaimed. "And who's the only one that can do anything about it? Ditch the boyfriend, apply for college and go get another job. It ain't going to happen by itself!"

They were just finishing up their steak and ale pie and house red – Helen wondered whether she should have allowed herself to be persuaded to have such a large one – when Theresa leaned over and said conspiratorially, "Kiddo, I think it's time to move on. You go and get in the car – here's the key. Be a love and stick it in the ignition for me and I'll be out in two shakes. Why don't you go out by the patio door, over by the Ladies – saves waltzing across the whole dining room." Helen didn't stop to think this was too odd at the time, and was just belting up when Theresa slipped into the driver's seat, a bit breathless. Gravel kicked up as she did an amazing three point turn to get out of the car park, and hurtled off in the direction of Frinton at a rather intimidating speed.

"Never let circumstances get in the way of your ambitions, kiddo," she laughed as she chose a rather circuitous route back to the village. "Now, I hope you don't mind, but I'm going to drop you off at the corner here instead of going up to the Green. I think I'd better get a move on." There was the distant sound of sirens as Helen moved to get out. "Theresa, thanks so much, you've been so inspiring and I wonder if we could . . ." but Theresa cut her off with a cheery wave. "Sorry pet, but I'm gonna have to shift – don't forget what I said and you take care!"

Helen watched in mute amazement as she spun off in a spray of gravel, pink hand waving from the window, and a mirthful laugh drifting through the evening air. She started up the road to the Bay Tree, feeling exceedingly light-headed and happy. When she entered the bar, her dad greeted her with a scowl, but even that failed to dampen her spirits and she slipped round the back to help out with orders. Alan came in just before drinking up time and accosted her with a cheery wave.

"Yo Helen, who was that driving JG's Porsche then? You are going to be a number one star witness far as I can tell."

"Why, what's up?" she asked anxiously. "That was Theresa, some relation of the Grants. She picked me up…why, what happened?" alarmed at the look on his face. He obviously had beans to spill.

"Well, we all know that the Grants are away at Cheltenham for the races." He stopped for effect, as Helen had clearly not remembered this. "And 'Auntie Theresa', or whoever she called herself, seems to have been havin' a bit of a joyride in their absence." Helen was speechless. "Shut yer mouth or you'll catch a fly!" Alan laughed. "Anyway take a look at this. I've just come back from town by the back road." He held up his mobile phone to show her a photo of a black car on its roof in a ditch, seemingly beyond redemption. "And before you ask, don't worry, here's another shot." He scrolled down to a picture of a colourful figure getting into a taxi. She was waving cheerily at the camera and, aside from a missing beret, looked none the worse for the experience.

"Message for you Helen. She said to tell you to get rid of 'the dead end, dead wood and dead dull.' I think that was right. Three deads anyway. Lucky she wasn't a fourth."

The next day Helen rose early. It seemed a shame to lie in bed when there was so much to do. Glancing out the window, she saw Terry's Towing Services drive by, a flattened black Porsche strapped securely on the back. Oh, and with a lime green beret just visible, caught up in the mangled frame.

WILDSONG
Catriona Tawse

Roddy poor thing. They found him at last, floating like a drowned seal among the Corragan rocks. Two frightened laddies racing for home to cry the news, the lurcher dog bounding behind. Gentle voices comfort the widowed mother, abject in her gratitude for the final knowing.

"Roddy poor thing," sighed the patient mother, old long before his late arrival, smoothing his wiry hair and taking the edge of her apron to wipe crumbs from the corner of the slack mouth. 'Hush you to sleep' and 'The cows at the milking' she crooned as he grew in size but not in words, only garbled utterances amid bursts and snatches of the tunes he heard in the world around. His music came from the slow air of a drifting cloud, the reel and drone of wind in the chimney breast, the crescendo of the tumbling waterfall.

"Roddy poor thing," murmured the quiet schoolteacher, guiding him through letters he would never comprehend, pointing the sol-fa notes black against the faded parchment. He learned from the birds, created his own modulator, the melody formed from the whirr of wings, the lift of larksong, the screech of gulls on the ebbing tide, no space inside his head for a clutter of words.

"Roddy poor thing," teased the young lassies at the dance, painting and preening at their little mirrors. "Am I your girlfriend? Will you give me a kiss?" Shuffling his feet in the Wellingtons he smiles wide and shy at the sounds of their tinkling laughter, bracelets clattering on skinny wrists as they clap to the swing of the Ceilidh Band, 'Bonnie Anne' and 'The Soldier's Joy,' the hall a heaving mass of heated bodies.

"Roddy poor thing," grinned the shinty boys on the bus home, giving him a fag and urging him to take a swig from the half-bottle going round. 'Caberfeidh' on the button box, a roaring chorus of 'Westering Home.' The symphony of the hard fought match still in his head, the clash of the camans, the snick and crack of the ball, booted feet pounding a rhythm on the withered grass and a shout of triumph going up for a goal.

"Roddy poor thing," sang the women at the Luaidh, brawny bare arms lifting and pounding the urine-soaked cloth along the weathered boards. 'Fil iu ro hu' and 'Hee ree ri o' he joined their choruses, swinging his own brown arms to the beat, unaware of the humour or the pain of the lilting verses.

"Roddy poor thing," grunted the men making for home in the boats, broad backs bending to the dripping oars. 'Pull her head round, now altogether' with water slapping off the bows, the mournful call of navigating geese muffled by the mist. 'Welcome to the Fisher Boys,' he is waiting on the pier for a big *scaithe* to take home. A last flap still in its tail, he hears the breath of its death song and comes near to tears.

"Roddy poor thing," nodded the dark-clad church folk, lifting eyes to the hills and psalms to the Lord in unhurried disunity, frowning lest his wordless voice be an intrusion, an insult to Heaven. Accepted for his innocence but unworthy of the Sacrament wine, he gives out the line in a way all his own, the minister's flat voice a strangely calming dirge. Floorboards creaking beneath respectful feet, polite murmurs of leave-taking then out beneath the open skies, the wind a banshee wail of release.

"Roddy poor thing," hummed the sea-maidens posing on the scaly rocks in hidden places of the Pilot's Cave, luring simple souls with melodies of haunting harmony. In the still calm of an evening he wakes and listens, the sounds tugging at the sleeve of his dreams till he knows the time has come. Into the gently moving waters he walks, pushing aside the clutching fronds, the voices louder now. Then down and dark, bubbles breaking and his glory gained.

"Roddy poor thing," called the searchers combing the seashore and dragging hooks through the Loch of the Stones in the dull gloom of winter's brief days. As hopes fade with each dusk, condolence and prayer bring little ease to those left stricken in their sorrow.

TRILOGY
Carol Fenelon

Silent

When you sidle in the door,
don't meet my eyes,
I know.
Silly grin on your face,
almost apologetic
but not quite . . .
defiant.
This is me,
this is who I am now,
you can't stop me.
This is the habit I have,
however hurtful.

I am not tolerant of
the hurt caused by
your great escape for
I learned as a child
to be watchful.
I am conditioned
to be careful.

I don't become drunk easily
Although I would like,
sometimes,
to join in the slow,
soporific,
laziness of it all.

I don't want it to be
like this.
I don't want to wonder
when you smile,
and are nice to me
if it is the drink
talking to me,
having got used to the
long,
painful silences.

Shadows

I know you have had
cancer.
I know the battles you
have fought.
I had thought that this would be
warmer,
safer,
more open.
I had not expected
the shut doors,
endless silences.

I have learned to live
without you,
by myself.
To draw on strengths
I never knew I had.
To live alone
with you.

To love myself
alone,
fleetingly,
with a faint sense
of distaste.

You have left me
already.
You have given to me
a funeral without a body
as you slip by me angrily,
furious at your demise.
still trapped,
carrying the seed
of your own destruction.

Kisses

I have forgotten how
we kissed.
Is that it gone?
The memories of
your tongue,
your taste,
your smile.
I do remember,
but it is enclosed
within a small space
to compress the pain,
to beat the knowledge
that it is gone.

I ache for your mouth,
running my tongue
over my lips,
tasting myself,
trying to remember.

TOOTHLESS BARMAID
L.A.Hollywood

Behind the bar, hanging between two mirrors, is a poster from the sixties of a young girl six feet tall in a sexy gold and black M&S bikini. She is leaning against a fake palm tree. It's in an oak frame. Hanging around it is a long piece of tinsel, the only thing to say it's near Christmas. It hangs there like the rest of the room, dull with age, with its ground-in dust and fag ash. She sits there on her stool behind the bar looking at the poster from so long ago when she thought she had the world at her feet. Then she looks around the bar-room with its dull woodwork, stand tables, patched chairs and benches. One hand holds her beer mug; the other hand rests on the bar and smoke drifts from a near-dead fag as she leans against the wall in her back-street bar.

One long look at the poster. Now she has shoulders like a full-back rugby player from lifting crates and beer barrels, to go with the ham-sized hands and broken nose she got from some drunk she had to sling out one Saturday afternoon. As she lifts her mug to the poster to drink to it someone laughs. She glares at the drinkers in the corner and slaps her beer mug on the bar-top spilling some beer.

No-one looks as she tries to remember what it was like to have a name that meant something so long ago. Now she sits alone and listens to old songs on a radio. The doors crash open as some drunk squaddie comes for a last drink before looking to pick up a tart for the night.

WE MIGHT BE LUCKY
Fiona Lang

She has been walking for a week, watching her feet and trying to make each step last. The only place she's going is the day she gets caught and taken back, and that's somewhere she's in no hurry to get to.

She isn't lonely because she has her own self to keep her company. At home she was always lonely. She used to sit hunched up inside herself, trying not to be heard, afraid to be seen. It was hardly ever safe to come out at all. Out in the open, she is out in the open.

Stumbling, she falls into the rough earth and straggling barley. Picking grit from her grazed hands and knee, there are no tears. Her hands are already scratched from picking wild raspberries, and her head is dizzy. She sits for a while, watching the ripe stalks sway, trying to store up warmth from the sun for later.

The sun doesn't last long. At the far side of the field the trees turn cobweb grey as a fine rain gusts in. She takes shelter under the hawthorn. The world is full of thorns and rain. She curls up, and watches the insects that tickle across her arms and hands. The rain quickly passes, but this is as good a place as any.

Beyond the hedge is someone's drying green and their house. She imagines a family, with herself as the daughter, and is disappointed by the woman who comes out with her basket and pegs.

"We might be lucky," the old woman says to herself, looking at the horizon. Her washing dances in the wind, and the little girl wants to run in amongst it. She wouldn't dare, but there is joy in the urge, which she has never felt before.

"We might be lucky," she whispers later into the dark, hugging her knees.

After several days the old lady walks into town. The little girl lets herself in at the back door and wanders into every room, hardly knowing what to do or where to go. She sits in the old lady's chair, drinking the sweet, scalding tea that she has made for herself, with tears running down her face. She can hardly swallow it, it's that good.

The old lady isn't surprised when she comes home and finds her asleep in the chair, dirty face tracked with tears and the cat cuddled in at her side. It wasn't the smudged nose prints on the kitchen window, or the pear drops that disappeared from the tin. It wasn't the posy of wild flowers on the doorstep, or the singing, or the handprints on her washing. She isn't surprised because the world has never brought her anything that she expected but occasionally just what she needed, even if she didn't know it till it arrived.

The cat looks up at her, wondering if this stray will be staying. "We might be lucky," she says, going to fetch a blanket and a face cloth.

THE WOMAN IN GREY
Frances Abbot

The young man came out of the mini-mart pocketing his cigarettes, turned in the direction of his home and stopped suddenly as if he had forgotten something. He did not go back into the shop again, but stood undecided for a moment or two before he walked on. His eyes were fixed on an old woman coming out of a doorway further along the street. He watched her hold back the heavy security door with difficulty while she tried to negotiate the steep step down to the pavement. She was small and wide. She clung with both hands to the door jamb, slowly lowered one foot to the ground and turned to face the door before taking her other foot off the step. The young man kept his pace slow. He wanted her out of the way before he reached the doorway. She was not done yet, for her shopping bag had caught between the door and the jamb. Only once she was free and the door clicked heavily into place did she move off, agonizingly slowly, in the opposite direction. He was glad. He didn't want to pass her. He quickened his pace, reached the doorway she had left, fitted his key in the lock and mounted the step. He manoeuvred the door with ease and bounded up the three flights of stairs to his flat. He let out a sigh of relief when he closed his own door behind him.

He had told his support worker about this disturbing neighbour of his. Living next door to her was the one thing he did not like about this new flat. Though situated above shops on a busy road, it was a quiet place. Everybody kept themselves to themselves and there were no children to plague him. Andy hadn't been very sympathetic.

"But you don't see her much, do you?"

"I have to pass her on the stairs."

He took great care to make sure she was not on the stairs before he left his flat. He stuck his head out the door and listened for the sound of footsteps. If he heard someone going up or down he went back inside until he was sure whoever it was had gone. He was a lot better with people than he used to be, but old habits die hard. If he did meet one of the other residents it didn't bother him much. It was only the old woman he felt he just had to avoid. It wasn't difficult to distinguish her footfalls from all others. They were heavy, slow, rhythmic, with many pauses while she stopped to rest.

"She's all grey," he told Andy. He described her from head to foot, grey wrinkled stockings, tightly buttoned grey coat, grey hat squashed on hair that had the look and texture of steel wire. She was grey. What he couldn't express was how this uniform absence of colour seemed to him to affect the space around her, spreading ever outwards like an infection to subdue the life force of whatever part of the world came into her sphere. In his mind's eye he saw her in an ever expanding grey bubble wiping out youth and joy and hope wherever she went.

"She's just old," Andy had said.

A short while later the young man was lying on the bed in his sparsely furnished room when through the wall he heard noises in the stairwell followed by muffled bangs and bumps. Something had definitely fallen or been thrown down the stairs. Should he go see? Somehow he knew, before he even peeked out of his door, what he would find. He was right; it was the old woman, lying in a crumpled heap on the landing. Just his luck. He knew that, much as he'd like to, he couldn't leave her lying there. Standing over her he saw her face clearly for the first time. He noticed her cheeks, slack and folded in wrinkles; eyelids fluttering over deeply set eyes; thin lips moving, trying to say something.

"Thomas."

"I'm not Thomas. I'm your neighbour, Jack. Can you sit up?" He moved to help her, but she pushed his hands away with surprising strength and opened her eyes to look into his.

"Get Thomas," she said clearly, "before he gets out on to the road." And she closed her eyes again as if the effort of speaking were too much for her. He found a large cat sitting calmly on the windowsill one floor down gazing intently at the people passing below. He gathered the cat in his arms. It was a warm bundle and made no protest at being carried.

"So, you're the culprit, Thomas." He had seen the scattered shopping and the old woman still dressed in outdoor clothes. The cat must have made a dash out when she opened her front door. She should have known she was too old to go chasing cats down stairs, he thought. It was no wonder she fell. She hadn't moved by the time he came back up, so, sitting beside her with the cat between them he took his mobile from his jeans' pocket and, only then, phoned for an ambulance.

Close to, now that he had time to study her, she seemed to have lost some of her power over him. Perhaps pity had dislodged it, or maybe it was because she smelled faintly of scented soap. He lifted the cold hand nearest to him, placed it gently on Thomas's warm fur and returned to his flat to fetch a blanket. She was awake by the time he returned. He saw her off in the ambulance with her house keys in his hand, wondering how, with few words and many assumptions, she had managed to get him to look after her cat.

He phoned Andy. "She wants me to go into her flat," he told him.

"You can do that, Jack."

"I suppose." He didn't sound too sure about that. "She must be senile, Andy, or I've got a very trusting face."

"Did you offer to take the cat into your flat?" Andy asked.

"No."

"Then you didn't give her any choice but to trust you," he said. "She's relying on you."

Still, it didn't feel right to Jack entering her place next day. He felt like an intruder as he inched open the door on the lookout in case the cat tried to get out again, but he found the tabby curled up nose to tail asleep on a cushion. Though he had been here yesterday to bring in the cat and the old woman's – he couldn't ever see himself calling her Elsie as she had requested – the old woman's shopping, he hadn't taken in much of the surroundings. Now, he stopped to look around.

In design and dimensions this flat was a mirror image of his, but there the similarity ended. He knew his flat was bland and featureless, the furnishings sparse and basic; only now he knew what it lacked. It had no life in it. Here, he could feel the old woman's presence in every inch of the space. The walls were papered over in a cover of amber and gold autumn leaves; the carpet, faded though it was, still showed the colours of its intricate pattern. Bookshelves were lined with the illustrated spines of paperbacks and a multi-coloured crocheted blanket covered the armchair drawn up to the coal-effect fire.

The room was small and crowded. It looked to Jack as if it were about to burst its seams for every surface held papers or books or vigorously flourishing house plants. Jack picked his way through to the table by the window drawn by the items he saw there. Set to one side were the paints, brushes and water jars she had used to create the little jewels of intense colour spread haphazardly over the surface. He lifted and examined one after another. Here were views from her eyrie on the third floor, the roofscapes, the river, the distant hills and here was Thomas in one after another glowing interior. Jack was enthralled. His hesitance gone he moved round the room greedy for every new sensation until Thomas's plaintive meows reminded him why he was there.

Each day after, as he turned the key in the lock, he told himself he was merely fulfilling his promise to the old woman, but each day he looked forward to the moment he stepped into her rooms and each day he stayed a little longer. From admiring her sketches he started leafing through books on art wishing he could cut out some of the pictures to pin to his wall. He began picking books off the shelves to take back to his room, but preferred reading them sitting in the deep armchair in front of the fire with Thomas on his lap. At these times he experienced a rare feeling of ease. The best of times he just sat and did nothing. He allowed himself to lower his defences and be comforted.

THE FAR COUNTRY
Sandra Bain

It was a sad little band left standing on the platform of the country station. They watched until the train rounded a bend in the line and was out of sight. They waited about, not sure what to do next. No one seemed in a hurry to return to an empty house.

The advertisements had read: *CANADA Opportunities for young men and women. Land available.*

Several young people of the small community had been attracted by the promise of a better life.

That evening instead of going to the pub for his usual pint Jock sat in the house and mourned. Canada had already swallowed up four of his children and now another son and Kate, his youngest daughter, were away. He didn't even know where Canada was . . . somewhere far to the west and more than a week to get there.

June 4th 1926. Today Dave and Kate sailed at 2 p.m. on the Metagama from Glasgow bound for Montreal. Left home 3rd June.

It was quiet that night in the pub. The innkeeper felt as though the world had stopped.

"I wonder did it leave on time." Jock was the first to break the silence that had descended.

Another man looked up from meditating on the contents of his glass and addressed Jock. "How far'll they have gone by now?"

"Oh, man, it's a long way to go," muttered the innkeeper and then with his usual lack of tact added, "I don't suppose you'll ever see them again!" Old Jock shivered.

"Yes, it's a long way," he responded. "But when they make some money they'll come home again." The man's sceptical look annoyed him. It was all right for him. His two sons had secure employment and were married with children. No danger of them going off to the other side of the world.

"Do you think they'll come home soon?" Someone eagerly caught on and Jock regretted the words that raised his old friend's hopes. Deep down he knew it was just wishful thinking. "You know, I can't believe that they've gone. Those wee lassies of ours are only sixteen. What does the future hold for them?"

Jock's only reply was a grunt. He didn't know the answer and he didn't want to think about it.

"They'll probably get married and settle there." Jock pondered the remark. What would wee Kate do if she had a bairn there in a foreign land without her Mam to help? It struck him then that he might never see his grandchildren.

Just then the noisy entrance of the boys from the Mains bothy shook the older men out of their morbid reveries. These boys were content with their lot. Not for them the rich lands of Canada. Their main ambition seemed to be to win the affections of the bonniest servant at the Big House and then settle comfortably into married life in one of the farm cottages.

"Well. Did they all get away yesterday?" Young Duncky quizzed. Those present knew that he was disappointed about Jock's Kate deciding to go off abroad with her brother. He had even tried to talk her into changing her mind. "Will they be able to send letters home?" The older men felt sympathy for him. It was unlikely that the lad would ever hear from Kate.

"I must away home, now. Goodnight, all." Jock hurried out the door before the tears ran down his cheeks. He had not much time for Duncky but at that moment he would have been delighted if Kate had married him and settled in a cottage at the Mains.

Seeing the smoke from his own chimney he felt a twinge of guilt. He had left his wife alone with their youngest child and gone to seek consolation drinking with his friends. As he wandered up to the door he calculated that in another five or so years the young lad would be old enough to follow the others. It was a distasteful prospect but he would never try to stop him – that would be like trying to harness the wind.

It was January 1932. Across Jock's coffin, his youngest son, now sixteen, looked at the anguished face of his mother. In that instant he knew that the far country was not for him.

SEPTEMBER SONG
June Munro

On a warm September evening I saw the bathers in the lake outside my house. I always sit there, in the chair by the window, the French windows open and the sun streaming across the verandah. The house is wooden, built in the Scandinavian style and blends in perfectly with the trees surrounding it. It began as an escape from city life and is now my haven and in fact my prison.

I can hear the buzzing of the insects, the rustle of the leaves on the tall pines and weeping birches that surround the garden and peter out towards the shoreline. They say that the lake was once part of a vast forest and its remains can be sometimes seen beneath the water. It is a dark, rather forbidding stretch of water and I cannot remember seeing anyone swimming there before. In the distance I can hear the cars, farm vehicles and trucks on the other side of the lake.

The scents of jasmine, old roses and lavender from around the verandah rails drift in on the evening air, and I wonder if there can be anywhere half as beautiful as here.

The lakeside is popular with picnickers and fishermen and they sometimes wave or call out greetings to me as they pass by. I always smile back, but they seldom stop to speak and that pleases me. Over the years I have become more reclusive, content with my own company, needing to speak less and to observe more.

I find it difficult to move these days. My companion is very good and patient; she needs to be, for I am dependent on her for the simplest of tasks and movements. My nurses come in twice a day, to get me up in a morning and to put me to bed before it gets dark, and in between I have Lucy to help me with my movements, to feed, water or change me, or to settle me to rest. Lucy and I have never formalised our relationship, feeling we had no need of any official sanction for our love, but now I do wonder if it would have been safer for her to have had a legal status in my life. She still seems to care for me as much as ever, but pity is no compensation for the passion we once shared. The winter days are short and the nights long but in summer the reverse, and I feel more alive and amongst the living.

The evening I saw the bathers was warm and sultry. The lake looked inviting, shining in the evening sunshine, and I too felt the urge to dip into its enticing water, but how could I? Even with Lucy and both my nurses the walk to the shore would be beyond me. I watched the four cavorting in the shallows. They didn't see me, being much taken up with themselves shrieking with laughter and splashing each other. The girls were both very pretty, one dark and slender, the other plumper and fair. The boys both had the slender athletic build that I had once had, they must have been nineteen or twenty at most, teasing and flirting with each other as they frolicked in the water. I felt a tinge of envy for what they could do and I could only watch.

They began to swim towards the centre of the lake fanning out in the water so that it became difficult to see them all without turning my head. I don't turn my head a lot as any attempts seem to reduce it to a football with a mind of its own, and moving my body myself is impossible. I kept the two swimmers in the centre of the fan in view and when I saw them coming together and looking anxiously about them, I realized something might be wrong. I heard them call out names, but could not make out what they were. The other two must have disappeared. All looked peaceful. The birds were still swooping and diving over the lake, the trees still rustling in the gentle breeze, but the atmosphere had changed. Fear crept up my back. My emotions are quite intact, you see.

They both started to strike out for the shore, coming towards me in what looked like slow motion. Then one slipped beneath the surface and the other one didn't notice at first. Then she realized what had happened and struck out again for the shore.

A moment later she spotted me and called out, "HELP! Please HELP." I kept looking at her, willing her to make it to the shore. "Help! Help!" she called again, weaker and more desperate this time. I continued to look straight at her, trying to let her know by the intensity of my gaze that I was doing all I could. They say that just off shore the lake bed is a mass of old trees and reeds and I think she must have become caught up in something, because she began to falter, to thrash about pitifully, and then with one final burst shouted, "Bastard," and sank beneath the water.

Lucy returned from the village an hour or so later, shocked and somewhat tearful.

"There has been a dreadful accident she said. "Four youngsters missing in the lake. A lorry-driver saw them from the far side of the lake but it was another ten minutes or so before he could find a house to raise the alarm. The police and all the boat-owners in the village are out now, but so far they have only found one body. Isn't it awful? I wonder if anyone saw anything."

She has become so used to my silence and passive presence that she clearly doesn't feel I could possibly have anything to add to the tragedy. Where is my voice? How can I tell her that I never want to sit here again? How can I explain what it feels like for a dying shell of a man to watch four healthy young people die whilst he remains a silent witness to their fate? That is my punishment.

SUMMER-TIME
Christina Macdonald

Dawn slipped in on silvered feet
While I in leaden slumber lay.

I knew it not but Summer-time
Already had begun the day.

No birds yet stirred, but as gold light
Began to lift a pewter sky

The feathered choir began to sing
And brief night vanished with a sigh!

A WISH WITH WINGS
Henriette A.O. Stewart

She flies between the sky-high buildings. Fast, swift, not afraid of the concrete hardness when she swoops round the office blocks' razor-edged corners and glides down crumbling alleyways of poverty. Her shadow sweeps through the streets of indifference, glides along walls of greed, briefly caressing the throngs of hard elbows.

The sky is surprisingly clear today; the sun shines down on rich and poor alike, and on her back as she flies silently through this city of anonymity.

She has a purpose, a mission. She is strong in spite of having sprung from the tiniest innermost corner of her creator's mind. She is a wish. An inspired and wonderfully pure kind of wish. You don't get many of those nowadays. No, nowadays wishes are whimsical and pathetic, made and then forgotten, left unfinished and unfulfilled in that no-man's land between daydreams and nightmares. Nothing flies from that sludge.

This wish, however, flies, and she is nearing her target. She slows a little, goes a little lower, circles the building three or four times. Well I got dizzy and lost count, and then she slides, just like that, right through a first floor window. I, being a body-bound creature, cannot go through closed windows, so I naturally slapped right into the glass and fell to the pavement in the street below. I should have known a ride as exhilarating as that would end abruptly. I'm fine by the way, just a headache and a sore backside.

I waited outside a long time. It began to grow dark; streetlights flickered as they were switched on and the city put on its nocturnal orange cloak. Suddenly the front door of the building opened and a group of people came out, springs in steps in spite of the lateness of the hour, talking animatedly, shaking hands, some even hugging. She, I couldn't see, so I guess she came true. She must have found an open mind at her destination and I suppose I do feel privileged to have seen supernaturalism at its most hopeful and promising, but I must admit I'm also a bit peeved that I'll now have to walk all the way back home. Perhaps I can hitch a ride on the back of a promise or a prayer. They are not nearly so fast; they are usually shackled with guilt and regret, but there are more of them and they will get you home, eventually.

THE ROBIN
Reg Holder

The cemetery lay quiet and undisturbed with sunlight dappling across the headstones. Some were old and grey, others new, shining in black marble with deep gold lettering. Nearby the small church stood, facing northwards up the Strath, for many years the spiritual guardian of its congregation and central to the lives of those in the locality.

The young couple opened the gate and strolled through the orderly rows of graves. They were from Canada and as with so many of their forebears had roots in this the old country. Their quest was to find the resting place of his great uncle whom they had never known but whose tragic story had oft been told and was part of the family history into which Shona had married.

"Here Angus, look! This must be the one. I'm sure it is." She called to her husband. Coming across, he looked down at the weathered stone; its lettering though faded was clearly visible:

Neil Macdonald
Tragically called
Always remembered
1906 to 1923

It was a miserable dreich day, grey overcast sky and a Scottish mizzle that crept into one's bones. The Reverend Angus Macdonald looked at his new manse and not for the first time was unsure if he had made the right move. He had accepted the invitation to become the new minister in the Strath after his beloved wife had died in the remote parish on the west coast that had been their home for all their married life. He could not bear to remain there without her after so many years and he knew that he must now move away from his present living and make a new start.

Freshly ordained into the Church, he had taken her there as a young bride where they had settled into their new life, raising the family that soon came along and becoming much loved by the folk that he ministered to. During the years he had been offered other livings, bigger and richer parishes, but they had resisted the temptations and saw no reason to leave a part of the world that they had come to love with all of life's joys and sorrows.

They were especially needed during the terrible war that befell the nation. So many lives claimed and so many of the young folk in the parish lost and whole families torn apart. They had been no exception, with the elder of their three sons killed on the Somme. Afterwards their second son, seeing no future in that place, emigrated to Canada, leaving only Neil their youngest born. He left for university soon after his mother was gone, leaving his father on his own.

And now, as he drove up to the large grey building of his new home, his heart sank and he feared for the future. Surely he should have listened to the entreaties of his parishioners who pleaded that he should not leave in his hour of need. Indeed, he had spent many an hour at his bedside before retiring, praying to the Lord for guidance but had received little help, and thus with a sore heart had decided that he must move and make a new life.

Mrs Mackenzie, the wife of the Session Clerk, emerged from the Manse, waving to him with a smile.

"Come away in, Minister, the kettle's on and I'm sure you will be looking forward to a cup of tea."

His spirits rose and moving gratefully into the kitchen he was soon in conversation and receiving first hand news of his new charges.

In time he came to know his new district and those that lived there. They were kind folk who had all suffered the ravages of the war and there were few young men to bring the crofts back to life, so many had left the area to look for work further south. But somehow the timeless rhythm of life continued. Winter passed and only Old Roddy, as he was known, had not survived the cold days. He had been well known and his funeral was attended by a large number of the congregation. The wake afterwards gave the minister a chance to meet many of his parishioners and he was comforted, even at that sad time, by how welcome he had been made.

As spring turned into summer his son, fresh from leaving university, came to stay. Neil loved his father and had determined to stay for some time before joining the firm of solicitors to which he was articled in Edinburgh. He made friends with the neighbours, a crofting family near the church, and Duncan Ross was grateful for an extra pair of hands to help with the work. They could not afford to pay him a proper wage but made it up in kind with eggs and produce from the croft. In truth, Neil did not mind. Fiona, their daughter, was always around and when work was finished, her mother would disappear after a suitable interval with the injunction that his father would be looking for him and not to stay too long. Sometimes there would be a Ceilidh in the village hall and the two would enjoy the dancing and the opportunity to hold hands with the promise of a kiss on the way home.

The day that the disaster visited them began in an ordinary way, though the clouds were dark and full of foreboding. The wind began with a whisper through the trees and then rose in fury, a summer storm that came from nowhere but lasted long enough to bring torrential rain, filling the river along the edge of the croft to full spate.

Neil, arriving at the croft, was met by Fiona with the message from her father to hurry to the river to help with a sheep that had fallen in and was tangled up in the bushes on the edge and in danger of drowning. The two of them raced through the blinding rain, to find that Duncan had slipped down the bank and was desperately clinging to a tree branch in the roaring current

"For God's sake, Neil man, get me out of here. I can't hold on much longer."

Without thought Neil slipped down the bank and grasping him around his body, slowly fought to bring him to safety onto the riverside. Duncan, by now overcome, had lost the strength to contribute anymore to his survival and, totally exhausted, lay half on the bank without movement. Fiona, unable to help but surmising her father was in mortal danger, ran back to the house to summon assistance unaware of what was to come. Neil, reaching down for a last effort, lost his footing and in an instant was torn away by the current.

It was two days before they found him, broken and bruised, almost at the river's mouth. The whole community was shocked and full with grief for their new minister who was enduring the loss of yet another of his family. Fiona mourning for a love that had yet to come to full fruition but one that they had known would be theirs for ever.

And so, in the low grey scudding sky, the church was again full, Angus taking only the second funeral that he had to conduct in his new parish. The pain was almost unendurable and he could hardly bear to even enter the church but he would not allow any other to undertake this last sad duty.

As the low strains of the final hymn flowed out of the church and down the Strath, a robin flew through the open door of the church and alighted on the organ just as the clouds broke and sunlight streamed through the side window, bathing the whole church in golden glory. And then at the end the robin flew upwards and, circling over the mourners, flew out.

"Oh Angus," Shona said, holding her husband's arm, "Just look at that stone robin on the headstone. I wonder why it's there."

UNLOCKING THE PAST
Jim Piper

My grandfather's three sheds have always been a mystery to me. In my early childhood he would say, "Now, young Missie, there are dangerous things inside." The old guy would spend hours in the main shed, and would wave to me out of the window. The muffled sound of music from his old transistor radio could just be heard and sometimes he would sing along. At other times the noise of electric drilling and sawing was followed by the hammering in of nails, which all sounded like an eccentric symphony. When he finally emerged I would ask him, "What are you making, Grandad?" And he would reply, "A whatsit for a thingamybob with wheels that turn backwards," as Grandads do to tease young ones, especially an only grandchild, a girl. Had I been a boy would I have been initiated into the mystical world of sheds? Who knows?

Granny, on the other hand, always used to say, "I don't know what he keeps in them. Mostly junk, if you ask me." But when something needed to be fixed he usually managed to find a piece of wood or some screws to do the job. She would say to him, "Arthur, that chair is all wobbly," and he would check it over, and say something like, "That's a glue job," or, "Wood's rotten. I'll make a new bit."

The sheds were painted every four years in the summer. The smell would linger for a week, a cross between a newly-tarred road and Brands Hatch. He hardly ever wore rubber gloves and would spend ages in the bathroom trying to get the grease off his hands.

His overalls were more a uniform than a concession to cleanliness and were not allowed in the house. He would wash them twice a year in an old galvanised baby-bath, then hang them from a tree in the garden. And so the old sheds had stood for fifty years or more. We are not certain of their exact age. He still had a big box of assorted ironmongery that was his father's and could tell you which jobs they were left over from, and say, "That door lock was only ten shillings and they are over thirty pounds now and not as strongly made."

So, on a warm spring morning in late March, I picked up the house and shed keys from the solicitor after both grandparents had finally passed away. The old shed keys had lost their shine having not been handled for a number of years now. The main shed had a large brass padlock and a door lock. After opening both, I prepared to enter the unknown. I said a silent prayer for Grandad and opened the door and, like unwalling some ancient Egyptian tomb, a shaft of sunlight shone down on to the bench illuminating the vice. It was almost a Stonehenge moment. Should I dance around holding a hammer or sacrifice a nail on a wooden block?

Everything inside was so neat. To the left was a shelf on which stood boxes marked 'split pins', 'A F nuts and bolts' and 'plain washers steel'. Under the shelf jam-jar lids had been fixed so that jars full of screws or nails could be screwed up to them and it was easy to see their contents. Just above the bench and below the window hung hammers, pliers, screwdrivers and spanners supported by nails knocked into the shed wall. An old angle-poise lamp stood to the right on the bench. A magnifying glass hung near it. This was like Grandad's own operating theatre to give surgery to worn-out mechanical and wooden objects.

I myself work in the fashion business. I have never hammered in any nails in my life – only filed and painted them. The fashion world and sheds are worlds apart. A cabinet on one end had old tins of paint in it and an old biscuit tin full of paintbrushes and sandpaper. On the back wall hung Grandfather's old bicycle. He rode it to work before he got the blue Morris Minor traveller, the badges from which were hung on nails above the door – an AA badge and an Advanced Motorist's badge. I can remember going on holiday in the old blue 'Morri' as he called it, roof rack loaded up with suitcases. What would he make of Missie's shiny pink BMW?

I left this shed and went to the garden tool shed. This one only had a small padlock. Inside the gardener's grotto were pick axes, one big and one small, various rakes, hoes, spades, and forks. Hung up on one wall was the old metal watering can with which I helped him water the rose beds on summer evenings. The large black hose on a reel stood in the corner. This was used mainly for washing the Morris and hosing its underside and ritually cleaning the engine compartment. The third shed had been the old coal-shed before they got oil-fired heating. Opening the door, there under a waterproof cover, I unearthed another treasure of past days. It was a sixties Lambretta Motor Scooter which Granny had ridden to work at the clothes factory. The chrome and the paintwork were in excellent condition.

I decided to put up a small shed in my own modest back garden. Inside I made a little shrine to Grandad which consists of his tin of old nuts and bolts, his old Morris Minor workshop manual and above it a picture of the old shed-man himself in his overalls.

There is room for the scooter and on sunny summer days I become a *scooterist* and go for trips out in the country.

THE SHAPE-SHIFTER
Fiona Lang

A t one time she was a young deer stepping nervously through the woods, and then for a while a wildcat, until she was tempted into domestication. She built a home for her children, by ceaseless toil and industry, which eventually they began to treat as little more than a lodge. Look what you have become, her husband says, such a fat and dull creature, beavering away. He doesn't recognise her as a native species. Dam, she thinks, and takes to a health and fitness regime.

Scurrying here and there, growing smaller and faster, she can eventually run straight up a tree without stopping for breath. Has she taken things too far, she wonders, but it's so exhilarating. She spends most of her time in the trees, the ones she didn't fell, on top of the world until one day her husband comes home and asks where his dinner is. Nuts, she shouts, twitching her bushy grey tail at him. You're not welcome here, he rejoinders, you aggressive and bullying invader. We only want the gentle reds here, with their beautiful, tufted ears.

Worried, she runs to the salon, where the stylist smirks. All the ladies of a certain age seem to want red hair. Next she will be taking up salsa dancing; a classic middle age crisis. She doesn't think it's such a bad idea, and that night she dances all the way to the end of the garden and into the woods of her youth, where she runs wild, before sloping home panting, with her tongue hanging out. Fox, says her husband, which she takes as a compliment until he aims a gun and fires.

For a long time she wanders, feeling very small, nibbling hungrily at the ground. Her nose twitches, alert for any sign of affection. A stoat finds her, and dances hypnotically so that she forgets to run away. He pounces.

What shall she be now? What use is an empty rabbit skin with the insides taken out? She resourcefully pads herself with whatever she can find; hobbies and interests and the music that the young ones like.

She joins a dating agency, but finds only other empty people and a few wolves dressed as sheep.

So she hangs herself on a branch and lets the wind dance her about, this way and that. Her children find her embarrassing, until the hobbies and music fall out of her. In winter her hide freezes solid, the rain soaks her, and the sun dries her out again, until she shrinks into a new shape. This is the best one she's ever been in. She is tiny, but fierce; perfectly adapted for life on the run. A shrew is too bitter to make a meal of, and she has poison in her bite.

HIGH HEELS TAPPING
L.A. Hollywood

Bridget comes down the street still
dressed from the night before
sparkly blue mini dress, short silver jacket
head thumping each time her heels
hit the damp ground, tap tapping
with each step taken.
Clock strikes nine.
Oh God, she thinks, they're all there the
whole village looking at her.
Her mum and dad try not to look at her,
her mum in a new long dark green
skirt and grey blouse, next to her
dad in his new grey suit, dark blue
shirt and bright, white dog collar.

MOONLIGHT SONATA
Christina Macdonald

Christie couldn't sleep. It was now after 5a.m. and still the moonlight streamed through the bedroom window. The curtains were left open so that when the time came she could catch the first streaks of light over the Black Isle, bringing in the dawn.

All was still, except for the occasional sweet wittering of a robin. The sky was a pale grey, lit only by a cluster of street lights below. All the windows round the Crescent were blind. No-one else was awake at this early hour.

She was vaguely aware of occasional soft, muted sounds of a car descending the steep brae. In old age, she had long forgotten the pressures of conforming to the discipline of work, the summons of clock and bell in the fur-tongued dawn.

Many nights she'd lain awake in the darkness, so many memories floating in and out of her mind. She tried to blot out the bad ones, the worrying ones, but when you are lying alone it's not always easy. She drifted in and out of consciousness, enjoying the warmth and comfort of the double bed, able now to stretch herself across its width, without restriction, without consideration for another body breathing beside her. Through a gap in the curtains a pale shaft of moonlight lit up the room.

The sight of her glasses on the bed-side table irritated her. They were one more piece of evidence of her increasing frailty, another sign of restrictions on her physical freedom. Her eyes closed and she drifted into the last reverie before the morning light invaded her room.

She was eighteen now – eager, fresh, still at school and full of anticipation of the world ahead. In a few months time she would be leaving the Island to go to university. Freedom beckoned enticingly – freedom from a loving but very disciplined home.

She was climbing the stairs now of the Old Seminary, her music satchel on her arm. She was sitting in the large room filled with curios. The room, once an old schoolroom, now filled with vases of flowers, old chairs, rugs and cushions, comfortable and dark were dominated by the presence of the grand piano. 'Grand' really was the word to describe it.

Her own old upright piano on which she practised had no style, just utility, occupying a space against the wall in the living-room, where there was little space or privacy to play. A piano needs space around it, the player needs space to make mistakes, to let growing emotions flow from the heart, down the arms, into the music . . . .

She was playing the 'Moonlight Sonata' now, the slow movement, with its deep lovely base notes. She had practised carefully at home but it was only now, in the big room with its exotic furnishings, the glass prisms catching the rainbows of light, that she was able to let herself drift down deeply into the meaning of the notes.

Christie knew that her teacher understood the way she felt. He had travelled the world with his music. He had played in Ireland for the aristocracy. He had even been to Russia! He knew when she pressed the foot pedal to sustain the momentum of the rich base notes, that the music echoed her deepest feelings, sublimated the teenage longings she had yet to express.

Christie slumbered on as the moon traced her gentle pathway across the dove-grey sky. At last, swimming slowly up through the depths of unconsciousness, she landed on the shore of reality. She had no piano now to play on, but still whenever she heard that wonderful music, she was transported once more to a land where bright dreams shone.

BRUADAR
Catriona Tawse
Translated into Gaelic by Anne Macritchie

Nach inns' sibh an sgeulachd dhuinn a-rithist, a sheanair? Am fear mu dheidhinn Eliza agus an t-each airgead."

Thionndaidh na h-aodainn beaga ris a' bhodach, aodainn a bh'air a dhol donn leis a' ghrian agus ceò iomadh teine, agus am bodach na shuidhe gu cadalach air bucas anns an robh innealan an stànadair. As deidh latha fada a' siubhal ràinig na Taisdealaich an làrach-campachaidh àbhaisteach aca, aig bonn Beinn Dìleas agus air an t-slighe gu Durness, aig ceann a tuath oir an fhàsaich. Cha d'thug iad fad' sam bith a' cur suas na teantaichean aca, an canabhas air a chumail le geugan challtainn lùbte. Bha cairtean nan laighe air na crannan aca, agus eich ag ith an fheur gu leisg, na h-earbaill aca a' priobadh air am bian dealrach aca. Tha àile còinneach dhearg anns an adhar agus tha cuileagan bheaga a' dannsa. Ann am blàths feasgar Samhraidh cha robh feum air an stòbh stain, bha prais stiubha crochaichte bho thrì-chasach air bruich le teine de gheugan agus mòine fodha.

Bhrùth Seanair an tombaca sìos dhan a' phìob aige, na malaidhean aige a' tighinn còmhla agus aghaidh cho stòlda, an aire aige gu siar far an robh an loch fada.

"'S ann thall a sin a chunnaic Eliza an each-uisge. Bha i a' coiseachd chun an loch le peilichean. Bha e a' fàs dorch agus bha pìos beag den ghealach ri fhaicinn air chùlaibh sgòth. Bha Eliza gu math eolach air an rathad agus bha i a'seinn fhad s a bha i a' coiseachd, òran Gàidhlig air call agus bròn. 'Obhan Obhan Obhan iri.' Chrom i sìos aig oir an loch agus lìon i na peillichean gus an robh iad làn uisge a' boillsgeadh le solas na gealaich. An uairsin, gun rabhadh sam bith, dh'èirich each glas a-mach às an loch air a beulaibh, a' srannartaich agus a' ràcadh an adhar le a ladhran mòra. Bha Eliza ga choimhead agus eagal a beatha oirre, leam an each-uisge thairis air na clachan mòra gleansach.agus sheas e a' plosgartaich agus air chrith ann am fasgadh craobhan beithe. Bha a ashròn ris an talamh agus amhach a' dol bho thaobh gu taobh mar gum biodh e air chall. Dh'fhuirich Eliza far an robh i, cha mhòr gun do ghluais i neo gun ghabh i anail, agus i a' feitheamh airson faicinn dè an ath rud a dheanadh an t-each. Chaidh a' ghealach air chùlaibh sgòth agus airson mòmaid chan fhaiceadh i càil leis an dorchadas.

"Na biodh eagal sam bith ort, cha dean mi cron idir ort. Ghabh Eliza iongnadh nuair a bhruidhinn an t-each rithe. *Thig an seo agus cur do làmh air bian Bruadar, each an loch.*

"Gun eagal sam bith oirre chuir Eliza sios na peilichean agus chuir i a-mach a làmh chun am beathach critheanach. Chuir i làmh thairis air a dhruim agus sìos aon slios, a' faireachdainn maras bàirneach. – mar bheathaichean a' gluasad fo a làmh. Thug i a làmh air falbh gu grad agus leig i plosg, a' suathadh na làmhan aice le gràin.

"*'S ann air sgàth deamhan olc bho uaimh air Cnoc nan Dall a tha mi mar seo. Cha tèid am mallachd a bhriseadh ach le cuideachadh bho mhaighdeann òg a tha a' dlùthachadh air a' ghealach agus e air tòiseachadh ag èirigh. 'S e seo a dh'fheumas tu a dheanamh dhomh. Thoir seachd fuiltean fada a-mach às an earball agam agus dean snaidhm Ceilteach asta. Cuir aon cheann dhe air mo chluais agus cuir an ceann eile air geug craobh caorann le dearcagan nach eil dearg fhathast.*

"*Gabh air do shocair agus nì mi mar a dh'iarr thu.* Le cridhe làn truais shlaod Eliza gu ciùin na seachd fuiltean, cho faiceallach 's a b'urrainn dhi. Bha i fìor eolach air fighe agus gu sgileil rinn i snaidhm achrannach. Chuir i an uairsin aon cheann den t-snaidhm air cluais Bruadar agus a' cheann eile air geug craobh caorann air nach robh dearcagan dearg, dìreach mar a chaidh innse dhi.

"*Nise seinn an t-òran a bh'agad na bu thràithe.* Le beagan crith na guth sheinn Eliza na briathran tiamhaidh, agus fuaim a cridhe na cluasan. Chaidh am beathach air chrith agus thog e gach cas bhon an talamh.

"Bha Eliza a' coimhead le iongnadh fhad 's a dh'fhàg na cùisean-gràin a bh'air buaidh uabhasach a thoirt air an t-each, agus iad a-nis a' dol sìos an t-snaidhm fuilt a rinn Eliza gu fìor bhonn an craobh caorann. Chaidh iad nan ceudan agus mìltean, agus nuair a thòisich bian nàdarra an t-each a' tighinn am follais, mhothaich Eliza gu robh e cho dubh ris a' ghual. Gu h-annasach cha do dh'atharraich dath a' mhuing idir. Chuir Bruadar a shròn ris an adhar agus dh'èigh e ris na neamhan le gàirdeachas agus furtachd. Dh'fhairich Eliza anail bhlàth air a h-amhaich agus thug e taing dhi airson na rinn i.

"Ge be air bith càite anns an dùthaich seo a bhios an t-sluagh agad bidh an còmhnaidh breac anns an loch agus bradan anns an allt. Agus dhut fhèin, tha do dhuais fhasthast romhad. Till an seo ann am bliadhna agus latha, agus gheibh thu am fear a phòsas tu."

Ghluais pìos fiodh anns an teine agus chaidh a' cheò gu ciùin suas dhan an adhar, fhad 's a thug Seanair an sgeulachd gu crìoch. Làn iongnadh, bha e follaiseach gun do chòrd an sgeulachd ris a' chlann.

"Agus a bheil cuimhn' agaibh dè thachair nuair a thill Eliza chun an loch as deidh bliadhna agus latha?" dh'fhaighnich e. Leig tè den chlann-nighean osann romansach, bha i cho eolach air an sgeulachd.

"A' feitheamh an sin air Eliza bha am fear as eireachdail a chunnaic i a-riamh na beatha. Sheas e àrd agus dìreach, chuir e a-mach a ghàirdeanan làidir rithe agus bhruidhinn e rithe gu sàmhach.

"Tha latha a' gheallaidh air thighinn, thuirt e. *Tha an geasag briste agus chan eil Bruadar tuilleadh na each, ach na fhear a tha airson do phòsadh agus a bhith còmhla riut bho seo a-mach.*

"Bha fios aig Eliza bhon a' mhòmaid sin gu robh gaol aice air am fear seo bho bhonn a chasan gu mullach a cheann, bha falt dubh air le srian geal, cuimhneachan air an ùine a chuir e seachad na each-uisge."

BRUADAR
Catriona Tawse

"Tell us the story again, please Grandfather. The one about Eliza and the silver horse."

Small eager faces burnt brown by the sun and the smoke of many fires turned to the old man who sat smiling drowsily on the box which held the tools of the tinsmith's trade. A long day on the road had brought the Travellers to their oft-used camp site kneeling in the shadow of Ben Loyal on the way to Durness in the northern tip of wilderness edge. Adept hands had quickly set up the bow tents, their canvasses drawn snugly over bent hazel branches. Unhitched carts rested on their shafts and tethered ponies cropped grass lazily with tails twitching over their shimmering skins. The scent of bog myrtle filled the air and small flies danced their brief life-dance. In the warmth of a summer afternoon there wasn't the need for the tent's tin stove to be lighted, a pot of stew hanging from a three legged tripod had cooked slowly over a fire of dry branches and peat.

Grandfather tapped down the baccy in his clay pipe, his dark brows gathering, his lined face serious as one arm waved towards the west where the long loch lay greyly asleep.

"Over yonder is where your aunt Eliza saw the *each-uisge*, the horse from the water. She went with pails to walk to the loch. The light was going from the sky but a wee slice of a moon came from behind a wandering cloud. Eliza knew the road well and sang softly as she found her way, a Gaelic song of loss and sorrow. 'Obhan Obhan Obhan iri.' She bent down at the water's edge and dipped the pails till the full surfaces of them shivered with reflected moonlight. Then without any warning a silver-maned head on a speckled grey body reared from the dark water before her, snorting and whinnying and raking the air with mighty hooves. Eliza looked on in frightened alarm as the *each-uisge* leapt clear over the shiny boulders and stood panting and trembling in the shelter of some thin birch trees. Its head hung low to the ground and its neck swung from side to side as if all hope was lost. Eliza waited still and calm with scarce a breath to see what the

53

creature would do. The moon was suddenly shuttered by a thicker blacker cloud and for a moment all sight was lost.

"*You need have no fear of me. I mean you no harm.* Eliza was startled to hear the words which came from the silver-grey horse. *Come here to me and touch the skin of Bruadar, the horse of the loch.*

"Eliza felt no alarm as she laid aside her pails and reached cautiously towards the trembling animal. She ran a hand over its back and down one flank feeling myriads of barnacle-like creatures rippling beneath her touch. She recoiled and gasped aloud, rubbing her hands in disgust.

"*An evil demon from the cave on the Hill of the Blind made me this way. Only with the help of maiden unbroken by man who approaches when the moon is in its early ascent can the curse be destroyed. This is what you must do for me. Pull seven long hairs from my tail and weave them into a Celtic knot. Let one end of the noose lie over my ear and the other round the branch of a rowan tree whose berries have yet to turn red.*

"*Be still, poor fellow, and I will do as you say.* With her heart full of pity Eliza teased out the silky tail with gentle fingers, tugging out the precious number with care. Long learned in the art of weaving she skilfully twisted the hair into an intricate pattern. Then she slipped one end of the loop over the ear of Bruadar and the other round the limb of a rowan where the berries had not yet turned red exactly as she had been told.

"*Now sing again the song I heard as you approached.* With only the slightest tremble in her voice Eliza sang the plaintive words with the sound of her own heart pounding a rhythm in her ears. The tormented beast shuddered and shook and lifted each foot in turn from off the ground.

"Before her astonished eyes the abominations which had gripped the skin of the *each-uisge* with such fastness were now scurrying in hasty disarray along the bridge of hair only to vanish into the hidden depth of the unlucky rowan. In hundreds and in thousands they went and as the true skin of the horse became exposed she saw how it shone with a blackness as if the night had closed around it. Strangely enough the mane stayed in contrast a silvery white. Bruadar raised his noble head and called to the heavens in triumph and relief. Eliza felt his warm breath touch her neck as he murmured his gratitude.

"Wherever in this wide county your people find themselves there will always be a trout in the loch and a salmon in the burn. And as for you, your reward is yet to come. Return to this spot in exactly one year and a day from this and you will find the man to whom you will be wed for all time."

A log shifted in the fire and a plume of smoke curled peacefully skyward as Grandfather brought his tale to an end. Wide eyed, the children acknowledged their pleasure with nods and exclamations.

"And do you remember what happened when Eliza went back to the side of the loch in exactly a year and a day?" he asked teasingly. One of the bigger girls heaved a romantic sigh. She knew and envied the tale so well.

"Waiting there for Eliza was the most handsome man she had ever seen. He stood tall and straight backed and held out strong arms rippling with muscle as he spoke softly to her.

"The promised day has come, he said. *Broken is the spell and Bruadar is no longer horse but the man who wants you by his side for ever from this time.*

"And Eliza knew from that moment that she loved this man from the soles of his feet to the hair of his head, his hair which was deeply black save for a white streak rising from his brow in an upward sweep, a lasting reminder of the time he spent as the *each-uisge*, the horse of the water."

UNTITLED
June Munro

When you were five and twenty
And I was young and gay,
We met and lives were welded.
We knew we'd never stray.

When I was five and thirty
Our family was complete,
Two sons, a lovely daughter
And life was oh so sweet.

When you were five and forty
Our lives, our love was strong.
Few cares we had or worries,
Our days were bright and long.

When I was five and fifty
The dark clouds hung above;
Your life was in the balance
We overcame, with love.

When you were five and sixty
Our tasks were all complete,
The work was done, the future bright
And life was oh so sweet.

And now I'm nine and sixty
And you are gone my love,
But memories live; they never die
You stay with me my love.

WINTER PASSES
Frances Abbot

It was time for the morning pill round. She was always first at the trolley. The other patients weren't too keen on mornings and she could generally count on a little time to herself once that ritual was out of the way.

"If you're going to the gym, Margaret," the nurse said, "how about waiting for a bit and taking Kate along with you?"

Margaret paused before she answered. She swallowed the contents of the little plastic container and said, "I'm not going to the gym this morning. I'm going out for a smoke."

"Better put on a coat then. It's perishing out there." The nurse turned back to her charts and Margaret returned to her room. She would have to go out now. Even if she got past the nurses' station and out of the ward without being seen to be dressed for exercise, someone would be sure to spot her in the gym and she'd be caught out in a lie. She'd be lucky if it didn't come up in her next session with her psychiatrist. Despite the many months she had been here she still found the constant scrutiny hard to accept. She put cigarettes and lighter into her coat pocket and made for the front entrance.

The nurse was right; it was bitterly cold. She could feel the air bite at her face the moment the automatic door closed behind her. It felt good. It even tasted good. Despite having no gloves, no scarf, nor covering for her ears, she decided on a walk rather than staying huddled by the wall. She lit up, drew the belt of her coat tightly round her, dug her free hand into her pocket and set out for a part of the grounds where the snow had not yet been spoiled by footprints.

The grounds were quite extensive. She had looked at them often enough through the windows of the ward when she first started to become aware of her surroundings. It had been summer then and the view had been restricted by the trees in full leaf. She had watched autumn come and go, but it was only in the grip of a hard winter that she had felt able to explore the paths that she had seen gradually opening up to her.

Today she walked with her head down watching her boots sink into the snow, listening to the crisp crunch at each step. The day was bright; the air was still. There was little to disturb the silence apart from the sound of a car entering or leaving the car park. But for that she could almost imagine she was the only person alive in the whole world. She shivered. She must not think like that. She stubbed the cigarette out between her fingers, wished she could get rid of unwelcome thoughts so easily, and put the end in her pocket. But it seemed that one unwelcome thought led to another and Kate came instantly to mind.

She hadn't wanted to take Kate with her this morning. Kate's condition was improving, they said. That's why she had been moved to Margaret's ward. They could now coax her out of bed, encourage her to wash and get dressed, even eat a little. Kate complied with little resistance, took her medication, said few words. Mostly she sat in a chair, ostensibly looking at the television set, but Margaret, watching, knew that her eyes registered nothing of the world on the screen, nor the claustrophobic life of the ward. Her gaze was turned into the dark places within herself where the pain lurked. Margaret was both fascinated and repelled by the way Kate's fingers seemed to seek out and linger over the healed scars on the wrists.

She was startled back to her surroundings by the *thwup* of a pigeon's wings as the bird flew from a low branch just above her head, dislodging snow down the back of her neck.

"Bloody bird," she shouted after it. But she was smiling. She was outside. She could feel the sting of the cold on her ears, delight in the sensation of snow on her skin, drink in the beauty of a winter landscape. She turned to retrace her steps and stopped. There under the tree, poking their green stems and white heads above the snow, were three snowdrops. She was tempted to pick the flowers and hurry back to the ward to prove to everyone that winter passes and a new spring follows, but she decided to keep this delightful news to herself.

VALENTINE ON THE MARINA – PONDICHERRY
Reg Holder

I see you; young lovers
Eyes only for one another
Your hearts entwined at the start of life's journey
Strolling blindly along the pavement stones,
Unseeing, you pass me by,
Poor helpless wretch

Gnarled fingers
Reaching upward in mute plea
Mangled arms
Withered useless legs
Drag this broken body
That has never known
The solace of a woman's kiss or tender embrace.

You pass me by
Yet I forgive and wish you joy
I have only crumbs of kindness given
For the few coins collected
In scorn or pity, it matters not
My wretched life
Waiting for blessed release.

CAIA AND THE VOLCANO
Henriette A.O. Stewart

The camp lay downwind of the volcano when the wind blew in from the East. This morning there was a strong smell of sulphur in the air. The gentle wind was surprisingly mild for this late in the year.

Caia stepped out of the tent and screwed up her nose; she hated that smell and she didn't like this place. She was far away from her familiar forest and homesickness gnawed at her like an aching hunger. She didn't trust these mountains or the people who lived here. The sulphur in the air smelt like danger and the few trees and bushes which grew here were stunted, misshapen and unhealthy looking.

Her own home was the Nagguri settlement in the Northern forests. The Nagguri only came here once every few years to hunt and trade, and only the fittest and most able members of the community were selected for the expedition. Caia had been overjoyed when she had been chosen, but her joy soon turned sour when she was told she was too young and inexperienced to be part of the hunting parties and would therefore be expected to assist with the domestic duties of the camp.

It was nothing short of torture for her. She had to fetch water, gather firewood, tend fires, cook for the hungry hunters and help butcher and skin the animals the hunters brought back. She had no time for herself and even if she had there was nothing for her to do in this place.

To add to her troubles a youth from the settlement nearby had, for some reason, decided to attach himself to her and follow her around like a devoted puppy when he was at their camp, which he seemed to be all the time.

Dawkum was his name. He had brown greasy-looking hair and a big nose, and his face had an unsightly collection of pimples in various stages of maturity. Caia knew she herself was not very beautiful. She was short and skinny and her breasts were very small, but that didn't matter to her, she was not concerned about her looks. Dawkum's attention mystified and annoyed her.

Caia went round the tent to walk the short distance to the temporary dump for her morning pee, but as she rounded the tent she noticed that some of the people from the mountain settlement were already there, including Dawkum. Caia bent her head to hide her face behind her long black hair in the hope Dawkum would get the message that she didn't want to talk.

"Caia. Wait!" She began to walk faster. Dawkum caught up with her and blocked her way.

"I'm going to the dump," she told him, frowning at him through her curtain of hair.

"I have never seen your hair loose like this before," he said, lifting a strand away from her face.

"I really need to go, Dawkum."

"It looks so shiny in the sunlight."

Caia stood mutely where she was till Dawkum eventually stepped aside and let her pass. He walked after her all the way to the dump. Once there he went over to a miserable-looking little tree and proceeded to pee on it, not caring about the splashes of urine staining his foot leathers. Caia waited for him to finish and leave her alone. He took his time. Caia turned away and looked in the direction of her home forest without seeing it. Home was six days walk from here. A fresh wave of homesickness nudged her heart. When she turned back, Dawkum had finished but didn't seem to have any intention of leaving.

"Well then, go away," she told him.

"Why?"

"I don't want you to watch me."

"You watched me."

"I didn't! I was just waiting for you to leave."

Dawkum shook his head, grinning, and Caia felt a lump of frustration swell painfully in her throat. But she wasn't going to show him that it bothered her. She turned her back to him, pulled down her leggings and peed on the dry soil, feeling his eyes on the parts of her skin which she was unable to hide. When she had tucked herself back in she turned back to face him.

61

"What have I got to do to make you leave me alone?"

Dawkum gave her a longing, pleading look and was just about to speak when Caia interrupted him:

"Forget it, that's not going to happen!" She turned away from him and began walking towards the camp. Dawkum caught up with her and easily matched her fast walk with his long legs.

"Caia, listen, I will give you something in return, something nice, something pretty."

Caia stopped and looked at him incredulously.

"You think you can buy me like some man-pleaser?"

"No no, it would be more like a love token."

"Love? I don't even like you."

"But I like you."

Caia did a loud 'tut' and turned with a swish of black hair and continued her walk up to the camp.

The rest of the day passed for Caia with chores boring enough to turn her brain to mush. Her eyes were stinging from tending the smoke-fires that kept the flies away from the drying meat on the racks and her hands were raw from scrubbing root vegetables in the cold river. Whenever she finished one task someone would spot her being idle and promptly make her do some other mind-numbing, muscle-aching, finger-skinning task. She missed being able to slip away into the forest when she had completed a task, like she did at home, or even better; slip away before she was given any tasks.

Caia sat back on her heels from another task completed and looked up into the clear sky. The sun had left the camp a while ago but was still shining somewhere behind the snow-dusted mountains. The air was a lot cooler now and her breath turned to mist as she sighed. The smell of sulphur had receded and the air was still. Caia knew that the Nagguri would stay at the camp until the weather began to show signs of turning but, as yet, one glorious autumn day followed the other. She loosened her hair, shook her head and thought of what Dawkum had said about her hair looking shiny in the sun. Of course, there was no sun now and it looked as dull as ever.

Gathering her hair at the nape of her neck and tying it with a soft leather strap, Caia headed for the tent she was sharing with five other Nagguri women. Inside she flopped down on her sleeping furs and wished for bad weather.

Moments later one of the other women came in.

"Feeling tired Caia?"

"Hmf."

"Well, you are young and fit, hard work makes you stronger. When you are my age hard work wears you out." The woman sat down with a groaning sigh.

"I'm making mint tea Caia, would you like some?"

Caia heaved herself into sitting position and rubbed her eyes.

"Does that mean yes?"

"Mmm... yes." Caia mumbled.

The older woman found two cups in one of the baskets suspended from the canopy of the tent and put some sprigs of fresh mint in them.

"Well Caia, it's nice to see you working so hard. I must say I had my doubts when they announced that they were taking you along too, but I am very pleased to have been proved wrong." She pulled off her foot leathers with some difficulty and gave a contented sigh when they were both off. The bitter smell of sweaty feet began drifting round the tent.

"My feet are aching; any chance you would massage them for me?"

Before Caia had a chance to utter her disgust, someone scratched at the side of the tent and Dawkum's voice spoke:

"Are you in there Caia?"

The older woman looked questioningly at Caia.

"Yes, I'm here." Caia sprang up and nearly knocked Dawkum over in her haste to exit the tent. Dawkum was wearing a pack on his back and a secretive look in his eyes.

"Are you going to take this mint tea, Caia?" came a voice from inside the tent.

Dawkum stifled a giggle and signalled for Caia to follow him. There was something deeply compelling about him here in the luminous half-light and Caia decided, right there and then, to do what he wanted. She was 16 after all, she could make her own decisions. As she walked out of the camp she could still hear the older woman's voice from inside the tent.

"At least take your parka Caia, it's a cold evening… what would your brother say if you came home ill, he'd think we didn't look after you properly… Caia… are you still there…?"

Caia followed Dawkum silently as they walked away from the Nagguri camp. She was good at walking silently, good at paying attention to where she put her feet. Years of living in the forest had taught her to be noiseless. Dawkum on the other hand walked very noisily. His big feet slapped the ground with every step and he had an annoying habbit of making grunting noises at the back of his throat. The air had grown even colder now; Caia felt it cling to her skin. They were walking in the direction of the volcano. She looked over her shoulder at the camp behind them; the light from the fires was now a distant dull yellow glow in the darkening landscape.

"How far are we going?" she asked Dawkum's back.

He stopped and turned round.

"Why? You haven't changed your mind, have you?"

Caia had never noticed that Dawkum was so much taller than her. She shivered.

"No of course not, I'm still here aren't I?"

"You should have brought your parka like your mum said."

"My mum? That's not my mum. Anyway, I'm not cold. Let's just keep walking."

But Dawkum didn't move. His eyes were dark and serious. She looked down at her feet.

"You can have the under-sheet, it should keep you warm enough for now." Dawkum took his pack off and pulled out a big light-coloured hide and handed it to her. It felt soft and light, like a baby wrap. Caia threw it over her shoulders and felt warmer immediately.

"Better, yes?" Dawkum asked. Behind him, the volcano was sitting like a potent sleeping toad, looking suspiciously benign.

They walked up what Caia thought was an ordinary hill but as they arrived at the top it levelled out into a large plateau which had been

64

completely hidden from view lower down.

"Have you ever seen a hot pool before?" Dawkum asked her as he walked towards a large pond. Steam was rising from its surface like the misty witches of the marches.

"We don't normally bring visitors here, unless they are ill. I thought it might help relax you a bit." Dawkum walked over to a small circle of stones and began getting a fire going with the kindling he had brought along.

Caia wanted to ask him what he meant about helping her relax, but she knew. She knew she was standing on the last ledge before her leap into adulthood, knew that her last bond with childhood was about to be severed and she was glad. She wanted to get this over with. Why Dawkum wanted this was not at all clear to her. He obviously hoped to derive some pleasure from it and was willing to give her something valuable in return. She was just hoping it would be over quickly. Like getting a bad tooth pulled out.

She went over to the steaming pool and kneeled down by its edge. Slowly she put one finger into the water, then the whole hand. It was hot, almost too hot, but she kept her hand in, testing herself to see how long she could stand it. The heat didn't get worse. She grew used to it and after a minute it just felt nice. She immersed the other hand and shivered with pleasure as goose-pimples formed and grew up her arms. The crackling sound of wood burning told her Dawkum had managed to get the fire started, as did the orange dancing light from the young flames on the ground beside her. She could hear him moving about behind her as he erected a small tent. Soon he came over and sat down by the pool's edge beside her.

"You can go all the way in if you want," he told her. Caia withdrew her hands and pulled the sheet closer round her shoulders. She had no intention of bathing in volcano-heated water. Who knew what it might do to her. Dawkum was smiling at her, his face soft and smooth-looking in the firelight. He had something enclosed in his fist and he held it out and gestured for her to receive it.

"It's a rock crystal," he said.

Caia looked in wonder at the smooth transparent stone he dropped into her hand. She had never seen a gemstone this big. As it lay in her open palm, cold as night and hard as rock, the firelight fluttered over its mirrored surfaces and penetrated its core, giving the impression it was alive. She closed her fingers round it and looked up into Dawkum's deep dark eyes.

"Come," he said softly.

She held the gemstone in her hand throughout; not that it lasted very long. Though Dawkum had been eager, he had also been gentle, and the dreaded barrier burst with less pain than Caia had imagined. Now the air in the small tent was heavy with human heat. Dawkum was fast asleep beside her, on his back with both arms above his head, still making those grunting noises in the back of his throat. Caia rolled away from his sweaty smell and put her newly acquired gemstone to her lips to feel its smoothness. It was as warm as herself now.

Caia didn't sleep much that night and was up and out of the tent before Dawkum woke. The sky was just changing from deep black to morning-time grey. While she peed on the dry pale ground she noticed that her moon-time seemed to have started already. She hadn't expected it yet; she was only halfway through her cycle. She went over to the hot pool and sat by the water's edge. Before long, the sky changed from grey to dull gold and she felt the wind pick up, not from the East as usual, but from the North, stronger and cooler than before. A loose bit of leather on the tent began to flap and smack in the wind and the noise woke Dawkum up.

"Caia," he called, poking his head out of the tent, "come back inside for a little bit."

Caia shook her head at him. She wanted to get back to her camp.

Together they pulled the tent down, Dawkum a lot more roughly than necessary, yanking out the poles and throwing them on the ground.

"Do you want to wear this again?" He asked tossing the soft light-coloured sheet at her feet. Caia bent down and shook the dust off it and threw it round her shoulders. Dawkum was looking at her, his eyes grey, and soft like ashes.

"Did you not like it last night?" He asked.

She looked away. He took a step closer and put his hand on her shoulder. She shook it off.

They walked in silence, Caia behind Dawkum. The wind was whipping playfully around them, rumpling Dawkum's hair and stealing up under the sheet Caia was wearing. The light from the newly-risen sun was soon blocked by an angry mass of dark clouds. Caia smiled, she would be going home today. She guessed that the camp would be packed up by the time she arrived, and hopefully one of the other women would have packed her things for her. She was still clutching her gemstone. When she got back to the camp she would put it in the pouch she normally carried in her belt. That would be the safest place for it. She had no doubt it was very valuable.

She broke into a trot to get up alongside Dawkum.

"Where did you get this?" She held out her cupped hand with the gemstone.

"What does it matter? It's yours now." Dawkum replied grumpily.

"I'd just like to know its value."

Dawkum looked at her, frowning. His grey eyes were darker now and sharper than they had been in the infant light back at the hot pool camp.

"I traded it, from a traveller." He finally said.

"What did you trade it for?"

"It doesn't matter." His voice was hard. He began walking faster. Caia was not put off, she could walk fast too.

"I'd just like to know if this kind of stone is very rare." She said.

"It's not common."

"But what value did you trade it for? I need to know if I ever want to trade it myself."

At this, Dawkum stopped and looked at her, eyes travelling up and down her body.

"What was the value of what you gave me last night Caia? The answer will be the value of that stone."

He reached out and grabbed her hand before she could withdraw it. The gemstone dug painfully into her palm as he held her closed fist tight in his. Caia looked up into his face, expecting to see that hard dark look in his eyes again but saw to her surprise that tears were rolling down his cheeks.

"You can find your own way from here," he spat and dropped her hand like it had burnt him. Caia watched as he half-ran down the path. She was fleetingly tempted to run after him but checked herself; she had done nothing wrong. Pulling the soft sheet over her head she gathered it tightly under her chin as she began walking in the direction of the Nagguri camp.

"Oh fine time to appear Caia, just when all the work is done." The older woman had obviously been looking for her.

Caia walked over to where their tent had stood and quickly found her back pack which had, as she had hoped, been packed for her. She pulled out her belt with the small pouch and put the gemstone safely away.

"You had me so worried when you didn't come back last night." The old woman followed Caia down to the small stream. Caia wanted to wash before the journey.

"Did you spend the night with that young man?"

Caia shivered as she splashed water under her armpits.

"Talk to me Caia, tell me you didn't do anything silly. Your brother will be furious with me if…" Caia bent forward and ducked her head into the freezing water and didn't hear anymore of the old woman's rant. When she sat back the old woman had stopped talking and was looking at her gravely, holding out the soft light-coloured sheet for Caia to dry herself in.

After dressing carefully so her moon-time wouldn't stain her leggings, Caia went back to what was left of the camp and found some cold leftover porridge and a piece of flatbread. It tasted wonderful. She helped with packing up the rest of the camp, stopping every so often to look in the direction of Dawkum's settlement and to check that the pouch with the gemstone was still securely fastened in her belt. She had rolled up the soft light-coloured sheet and stowed it away in her pack Surely Dawkum didn't expect to get it back.

Every time Caia looked back, the slumbering volcano had shrunk in size. Soon she would not be able to see it at all. The Nagguri had abandoned camp not long after Caia's arrival and the mood was high; most of the hunting expeditions had been successful and there had been many favourable trades made. They would be well received at home.

Caia turned to look at the volcano, for the last time she told herself, just as the first spit of rain fell on her face. The volcano was shrouded in low clouds now and she could no longer see it. A small sigh escaped her lips.

She turned away from the sleeping mountain, the rain intensifying as she walked quietly behind her group. She began humming to herself. The rain didn't matter, the heavy pack didn't matter, she was going home. Home to her normal life of roaming the forest, free as a fox, unrestrained as a lark. The only mementos she brought back with her was the light-coloured sheet deep inside her back pack, and, hidden away below the warm folds of her parka, the gemstone that was nestling safely against her hipbone.

THE SIGNMAKER
Louise James

When asked, Frank's response was always the same. "Nothing ventured, nothing gained," he'd reply in his broad West Yorkshire accent. "What do I miss – beside the footie, of course? I'll let you know when I think of it."

He and Sally took the decision to move north after a close shave, what he now refers to as his wake-up call.

"Damned lucky I didn't crash the car or lose my licence. I were doin' sixty in a thirty – million miles away when sommat caught me eye, swerved to miss a dog, but it could have been a kiddie. Got home and said to Sal, 'That's it, I'll get killed or kill someone if we can't cut the stress out of our lives'. People said, 'Why Scotland?' – that's before it got worse and they found out it's the Highlands – but I always say, 'Just redressing the balance a bit, mate, and after all I am a MacKenzie on my Mam's side'."

Of course there was bound to be a slow start. Signmaking tends to be quite a local business, so it took a good while to build up a client base, make himself known, and so on. Fortunately he and Sally would turn their hand to anything and they did, that first year. Sally used to run her own catering business down south but definitely wanted to move away from that line, given the unsocial hours and, of course, she no longer had her parents at hand to help with childminding. Now, though, she had landed a marketing job with a health food wholesaler and could work from home for part of the week so things were looking up on the financial front. Yes, all in all, the move north was the best thing they could have done.

Bit rough for the boys at first.

"Dad, what's a white settler?" Jono asked one day coming home from school. With only a second's pause, Frank replied, "Liverpool supporter, mate. But don't you worry; most lads have a Premiership Club up their sleeve as well as their SPL team. Maybe they'd like to see your autographed Liverpool poster one day. See how it goes first though. You don't want to find they're all Arsenal fans."

After helping out with a sign at short notice, Frank now found that the Council provided a steady stream of business. All signage had to be in English and Gaelic – this was the law, apparently, so everything new or needing replacement wanted doing. For most things this was very straightforward: entrance, exit, toilets – Gaelic words and phrases were already in use. But for the more specialist signs, (*slippery when wet*, *yoga for beginners*), you would think they would have thought this out and provided him with the Gaelic. But no, their chaotic ordering system meant he was always working to a deadline and last week no translation was provided for the job. Getting it done was not as easy as you'd think. Frank was no slouch; he was soon on the phone to Council trying to track down the person in charge of such things, but after a few wild goose chases he was getting desperate. He really did not want to be scrabbling around at the last minute.

On Friday he walked his youngest, Nathan, to primary school, and round the back passed the entrance to the Gaelic nursery. Aha! There were two mothers, propped on the low wall, nattering away – incomprehensibly – ten to the dozen with the janitor. Why hadn't he thought? He could get his translations done here. After depositing Nathan at his classroom door Frank approached the nursery teacher.

"'Morning. Mind if I ask a favour?" He hesitated. "I need some words translating into Gaelic for some Council signs I'm doing. Would I be out of order asking your caretaker there," motioning with his arm to the chattering trio, "if he'd be able to oblige?"

Mrs Wilson managed to look both bemused and amused at the same time.

"Now why would you be wanting to ask George about that? He's Polish."

THE LATE CHRYSANTHEMUMS
Christina Macdonald

The late autumn sun had turned the garden to gold. Yellow and bronze curved chrysanthemums stood, still and proud in the border lit up by the last lingering light of the afternoon. Angus, seated on an old kitchen chair by the back door, sighed with satisfaction.

His garden was his solace. Every spare moment was spent there, especially now since her death a few months before. He could still feel her presence in the home. At times it overwhelmed him, at others it was a relief that she was now gone and his life finally was all his own.

His conscience, he felt, was clear. He had cared for her over the years but she had been an easy burden to bear. Her gentle disposition had asked very little of life and she had given a great deal to the community of which they were a part. Her disability had not hampered her generous projects. He had supported her dutifully, played the subservient role, always in the background to deliver the harvest gifts of baskets of fruit she had prepared, the toffee she had made for various fund-raising efforts.

Patiently he had read out the titles in the book catalogues for the blind, carefully omitting those which he guessed she would find unseemly. As her eyesight had dimmed her embroidery had lain half finished in her sewing box, the half-crocheted blanket stored in a cupboard, her baking skills confined now to humble scones.

In turn she had encouraged him in his garden and was proud when he won small prizes for his vegetables and fruit Perhaps, too, recognising his vulnerability in forming relationships, she had realised that his affinity with his plants, which demanded no reciprocal affection, helped to fill an emotional need of which he himself was hardly aware.

There had been, occasionally, other women in his world, kindly, quiet, softly religious, who had made gentle approaches to him but with whom he had not experienced that fierce explosion of passion, the strong primal urge which true attraction to a woman can bring.

What he did not know he did not miss but recently he had felt his body ache for an unknown something -a feeling so alien to him he was afraid of where it might lead.

It had begun a few months ago, not long after his mother's funeral. He had made his dutiful way to church, accepted graciously the gentle condolences of those in the congregation whom he knew and those he did not, but found no consolation. His God had removed the being who had meant the whole world to him. He resented this though he was glad she had not wasted away with cancer but had been found asleep in her chair late one afternoon when he had returned from town. How could he fill the gaping void which now lay ahead of him?

He re-lit his pipe and moved the chair from shadow into a patch of sun by the west wall. All the plans he had nested upon in previous years began to hatch out in his mind. What to do with this vast and boundless prairie of Time which lay before him? He was merely skirting round the edges where it was safe, where the pathway was well-trodden, laid out, ordered. Beyond, looking over the fields of restless grain he could not as yet see a clear path ahead.

His gaze returned to the flowers, his beloved specimens, the fruits of his spring labours. He would pick them next week choosing carefully, colours that blended, for the Show. He'd exhibited many times before but this year, able to devote more time to them, a fierce passion to win the cup had begun to burn within him.

This passion surprised him. In all the years of suppressed emotion caring for his mother, he had never allowed his feelings a chance to surface. His sense of filial duty was so strong, strong since as a young man he had seen his father leave home for the sea and never return.

The pew across from him in church was occupied by a woman he had occasionally noticed when she was accompanied by her husband. She seemed a quiet little hen of a woman, he thought, inconspicuous beside her more flamboyant cockerel of a husband who strutted regularly into church in his yellow waistcoat and flashy tailored jacket. A year ago the cockerel had evidently succumbed to a heart attack and now lay stiff and silent six feet under, in the churchyard.

The woman had glanced across the aisle and smiled. He had returned the greeting and then lowered his gaze to the current psalm.

The following weeks, as he occupied the family pew, he had looked across the aisle and found her always there – a strangely comforting and secure presence. One Sunday he'd approached her as they left the church at the same time. She spoke kindly about his mother and enquired about his flowers and he in turn had asked her how she was managing on her own. There was no spark lit then but as time went on their mutual sympathy had begun to develop into a mutual need.

And today she was coming to visit him for the first time. He'd laid out the shortbread and fruit cake on the plate, the two best china cups on the kitchen table as his mother had always done. Now as the sun set beyond the garden wall he was waiting for her in the silence of the late afternoon.

At precisely half past four he heard footsteps on the path and the back gate creaked open. Mary stepped in diffidently, He knocked out his pipe and rose to greet her.

"Come and have a seat here for a few moments," he said pointing to the old garden bench under the kitchen window. Its paint was flaking off, he noticed, and made a mental note to paint it before winter set in. "You'll just be able to catch a few more minutes of warmth before the sun goes down."

She sat down carefully on the seat and placed her handbag neatly beside her. Opening it up she held out a small parcel done up with sellotape.

"I made you some tablet. I know your mother was a great hand at it and I thought you might be missing it." He beamed as she held out the package.

"Thank you. I'll just put it in the kitchen for now and while I'm at it I'll put the kettle on."

He stepped in the back door. Mary looked out over the flowers growing in profusion and wished her own garden was as pleasant as this. Her late husband, being of a practical rather than artistic nature,

74

had had the whole area laid out in slabs and woe betide any weeds which dared to poke through. The tiny patch of grass he had allowed to grow at the back had been manicured to perfection.

Mary noticed with pleasure that Angus had allowed a few wild flowers to inhabit his garden near the hedge and the birds were busily flitting to and from the peanut bags he had set up on the overhanging branches of his neighbour's apple trees.

"Would you like to come in now?" he said, wiping his hands on a kitchen towel as he poked his head round the door. She followed him into the kitchen and sat down at the neat table covered in a red checked cloth. The teapot was ensconced in the middle of the table wrapped in a woollen cover which resembled a thatched cottage. Mary thought about her own formal table settings when Malcolm had been alive and smiled with pleasure at the offering before her.

Angus poured the tea, handed her the cup with a formal gesture and then passed the sugar bowl and milk jug. "I'm sorry I don't have any home baking for you. Mother was always good at it. Her door was always open for her friends and her table always laden."

They sat without speaking as they drank their tea, an awkward silence suspended on invisible threads between them, neither as yet willing to be drawn into a closer web.

"When is the Flower Show?" Mary broke the silence.

"Next week," Angus replied, "and just as well because my chrysanthemums are just at their best now. I hope we don't get any strong winds before then." Their conversation continued in a stilted fashion about trivialities, neither wishing to seem to be probing into the other's life and yet eager to become more familiar.

She had spent so much time in the shadow of her showy husband she hadn't had the opportunity to express herself – an insignificant figure in the background – pale foil to his public career. Yet of the two of them, she knew she had been the stronger one. Many a time in the past she had had to shore up his confidence when his business had seemed to be in crisis and to be honest, he had recognised that strength in her and although he had seldom acknowledged it in public, she knew privately he had been very fond of her.

She looked on Angus with growing respect and quiet understanding. She recognised his actions, his diffidence, his awkwardness in an unfamiliar situation and warmed to him. It was said in the village that he was too tied to his mother ever to get a woman for himself but she recalled how tying her relationship with her own mother had been and how it was only after her mother had passed away suddenly that she herself had found the freedom to marry in her forties. She and Malcolm had had no children, nor had they hoped for any. It was only now that she felt an ache when she saw how happy her younger sister was, recounting tales of the exploits of her grandchildren.

Her thoughts were interrupted by the clock chiming. She glanced at her watch and rose to go.

"Well, Angus, I must get on now. I promised old Mrs Macleod I'd look in on her to see she takes her pills before tea. Good luck at the Show and I hope you'll pay me a return visit after it's over – with the Cup of course," she laughed. Angus rose to open the kitchen door and ushered her out into the soft evening darkness.

The following Friday he was up and out early to cut the chrysanthemums and carrying them into the kitchen, he carefully wrapped the curved heads in fresh tissue paper and laid them gently in the long cardboard box he had made for them. Just after eight o'clock he carried them along to the village hall where the judging was to take place. He arranged them precisely in the tall black vase provided, left the hall and made his way home again to await the results which would be announced by one o'clock.

The hours between seemed to drag endlessly. He could hardly suppress his excitement. He just KNEW these flowers were winners this year. He'd spent so much time with them, poured out on them all the extra care and concern which he had formerly lavished on his mother.

At the hall door his eager fellow exhibitors were jostling to get in first. Angus, hating any fuss, waited quietly until he was able to enter with ease. The floral exhibits in the various categories were a magnificent sight but he only had eyes for the chrysanthemums. He walked slowly towards the table. There, resplendent with a huge red rosette, stood his vase of blooms and beside it the Silver Cup.

Much later that afternoon, after a pint or two in the beer tent, the rosette pinned jauntily to his jacket and the coveted Cup tucked under his arm, Angus made his way happily to Mary's house, his heart filled with anticipation.

THE BUS
Reg Holder

There she stood, freshly painted and resplendent in all her glory. Holed up in downtown Jamnagar, Ranjit Singh had worked hard on the bus over the last few weeks and he had not allowed anyone into his workshop. This was a special job for his friend Mr Gopal Singh (no relation) and who knew what business that might flow afterwards? Not that he needed to advertise, for Ranjit was acknowledged to be the best in the district. Not cheap, but the best!

And sure enough Gopal Singh was delighted with the results. With pride he walked slowly round, taking note of the Swastika in the front to bring good fortune and to ward off the perils of the Indian roads and at the back the 'Horn Please' in lovely flowing curves and bright yellow colour. The rest of the bus was painted in various hues along the length of her body and bonnet.

Soon now she would be on the road and recouping his costs. Mr Gopal until recently had been plying his trade as the owner of one of the ubiquitous auto-rickshaws on the Dwarka road, and over the years carefully hoarded every rupee he could get his hands on. Sometimes this was to the detriment of his family life but he was determined that they would have a better one and nothing was going to stop him. It was hard though and at times he felt that there was much misunderstanding. Had not his wife that very week complained that she could hardly hold her head up with the other women when buying their foodstuffs in the market?

"Hai there she goes – the wife of a chakula driver, can't afford even the ghee with which to cook," they had scornfully said amongst other comments. This encounter bitterly recounted behind the *go down* in which they had some living space.

Well Mr Gopal Singh would show them. The big secret would soon be out. Yes there was the sign painted prominently on   the driver's door. 'Gopal Singh and Family' and underneath 'Transportation'. He had decided to include 'Family' in the name, which was slightly unusual. In fact he had considered just including his wife, but that was beyond the bounds of acceptance and the family had not arrived as yet. Another cause for considerable concern. But this would suffice for the present and would show those *bhindi bints* down in the bazaar.

Ranjit came to his side. "Isn't she beautiful? I know the sacrifices you have made Mr Gopal and so this was a special work for you. Soon I hope you will buy another and then who knows, Mr Gopal, you will be rich and famous and I along with you I hope."

Slowly the bus was wheeled backwards out of the shed into the street. Crowds gathered round, excitedly peering in to the interior. The driver that he had hired, dressed in a simple uniform but a uniform for all that, sat importantly at the wheel looking down at the pavement stalls and dilapidated shops. Yes, he too was on the way up.

And so they set off, first to the temple for the *Puja*, one could not be too careful and the Dwarka road was dangerous.

Afterwards to his house for a viewing by the neighbours – that would show them – and the first ride for his wife.

WET WEST COAST SUNDAYS
Carol Fenelon

Angus Peter poured the whisky into the glass, nearly up to the rim. Outside the rain splattered down the windows and ran in rivulets over the rotten paintwork. It was a wet Sunday and he hated wet Sundays – wet West Coast Sundays. At least during the week time could be filled with the potholes on the road to the lighthouse, trips to the Coop on the days the bread came in and measured by the graceful coming and going of the ferry with all its folks.

The great and the good walked purposefully past his kitchen window as he sat at the table he had had for the last ten thousand years seemingly. Solid oak, scratched in the middle and spread with the debris of his daily life – papers, letters, an old ring binder, a folder of old black and white photos. The great and the good wore their Sunday best. Sunday hats and dour Sunday faces with large Holy Bibles clutched under their arms.

Sunday faces for sinless Sundays then back to the usual on Mondays, he pondered as he sipped slowly at his single malt. Mhairi in the shop with a mouth as big as the Clyde tunnel and a mind on things other than stamps.

"Has anyone heard of a silent orgasm?" she had announced last Monday, stunning the queue for stamps and benefits into an immediate silence, eyes not meeting and leaving Roddy the Post rocking in silent mirth at the other end of the counter.

He threw the whisky over his throat and went to switch off his everlasting mince and tatties on the stove in the corner of the room. Both in the same pot, save the washing up, then back to his lonely station at the table. His book lay open, forlorn. He opened the ring binder and took up the biro with care. He had tried but still felt he hadn't written enough. She wouldn't read it anyway even when he had painfully transcribed it on to the computer. Letter by letter – word by word – thought by thought. There wasn't much he could say. This was not one of his mates with whom he had a daily gossip in the pub. This was not an idea, a figment of his imagination. This was the real world and he hated it.

He smiled at the photo of his wife on the wall. Well, she hadn't actually been his wife. Such a formality had never been got around to. His fingers touched her briefly and in doing so he remembered the taste of her – the way she had been with him – her softness below him with that gentle teasing laughter.

She had not been one for gossip, had kept her own counsel. This unwillingness to join in the daily comings and goings, that dissection of other people's lives, had labelled her as a snob. But she wasn't, he smiled to himself, remembering her belly laugh as they lay in bed and he told her stories of the sea travels he had made.

He missed her. This aloneness was worse than the aloneness on the ships that had been his home. At least, there, he'd had his letters but now there was only silence and the great empty space in his life where she had been his woman. He poured another whisky and crawled into his side of the bed, even though it was all his now. He lay and shivered until the warmth of the duvet wrapped itself around him.

He reached out and clutched the pillow to him. It smelt of her, faint and musky, her body warm and soft with smooth silky skin and as he imagined her there he felt himself grow and harden. He shook his head briefly, the ache and the wanting of her overwhelming him. He did not want to relieve himself. He wanted her to, but the emptiness in the bed was both the question and the answer. He glanced at the mobile beside the clock. He still left it on all the time even though he did not expect her to ring. It was too late for that now. He had fucked up well and truly. He lay quietly listening to his own breathing. From short and jagged he talked to himself, inside his head, until it became slower and steadier, quieter and smoother. He felt himself subside and was relieved. He had not wanted to do it himself. He wanted her. He turned onto his belly and lay watching the sky evolve gradually from the grey of the afternoon to the dark silk of the evening. Eventually, without trying, he slipped into sleep.

OVER THE EDGE
Sandra Bain

I opened my eyes and was blinded by the whiteness all around me. As I tried to focus, all I could see was snow, dazzling snow. I attempted to move but pain seared through my left leg which was twisted under me. My arm and shoulder had no feeling and my head ached. Why was the snow beside my face stained red?

Where I was or how I had arrived there I had no idea. As my mind adjusted, I could feel the shiny material of my ski jacket. I must have been skiing but where were all the others who usually thronged the slopes? Not another person was in sight. The snow was deep – no groomed piste here.

In spite of bright sunshine I could feel a cold wind on my face. I was desperately thirsty. Would I die of cold or of thirst?

If only I could pick up some snow. Perhaps I could move a bit. The pain was intense. Everything went black.

The sun was hot on the side of my face as I came round again. But I was still so thirsty. I turned my head as far as I could and succeeded in grasping a mouthful of what looked like clean snow. I didn't care much as long as it was wet. It helped a little.

I must move. I've got to move. I was feeling desperate. Little by little I turned on to my back. After that exertion I had to rest. The warmth of the sun felt good.

Feeling was coming back. One arm was unharmed and one leg seemed to be free from pain although with each movement I felt as though my whole body was falling apart.

Did I have a backpack? Mobile phone? I was coming to life and my survival instinct was taking over. Where were my skis? My ski poles?

If only I could sit up? I tried but it was painful and I flopped back down. I screamed. That felt better. I screamed again, and again. Was I hoping someone might hear?

I continued the struggle to sit up. I could now see around me. Nothing was familiar. Landmarks which I might have known were obliterated by the snow which stretched as far as I could see.

With my sound arm I tried to remove my backpack over the damaged arm.

What if I'll never be able to use this arm again?

I yelled out with the pain but at that point the strap came over my elbow and was free. Then came the task of opening the pocket which held my phone – fortunately undamaged.

Who do I phone? Mum, Dad, worry them? Let them know that at least I am alive. They could alert the police. There was no way I was going to get off this mountain by myself. *I'd rather die than try. Phone Joe . . . Joe? Why is he not with me?*

I always skied with Joe so why was I was alone*?*

Dial 999? I could hear the policeman giving a talk at school. "You could be in trouble if you call that number needlessly. There might be an emergency . . . ." *But I am an emergency. My thoughts were disturbed.*

I was beginning to feel sick and my head was spinning. I would have to lie down but *oh – the pain!*

How long I lay there I had no idea. The air was cooler and I knew that soon the sun would disappear behind the mountain and darkness would begin to fall.

In a moment of panic I tried to sit up again but the pain in my leg was too severe and I sank back.

This can't go on. I've got to get help. I fumbled with the phone which somehow had remained in my hand. I had difficulty finding '9' and my bulky ski gloves created a problem when I tried pressing the button.

I listened for the welcome tone, imagining the warmth of the telephone exchange and rehearsing what I would say when the brisk disembodied voice would answer.

But what can I tell them? I have no idea where I am.

Then came the bleep. No signal from my phone. I cried – and aggravated the pain.

What am I going to do? I might as well give up and die.

The sun was going down and the sky was darker.

It should be possible to activate the phone further down the valley. I could crawl. But with a broken arm and a twisted broken leg even crawling was out of the question.

Where is Joe? Why was I skiing alone? I must have been off piste. It's not safe. What's happened to my skis?

I asked myself the same questions over and over again before it occurred to me that Joe might also be hurt. He might even be somewhere near. I yelled his name but all I heard was the mountain echoing back . . . mocking me. I turned my head. The mountain behind me was dark and menacing with the sun now gone down behind it. The sky was awesome, streaked with red from the dying sun.

This could be the last sunset I'll ever see. I'll not survive the night on this hillside . . . unless I can get shelter, but I can't move. And there's no food . . . .

Then I remembered my backpack. I was leaning on it. My mind was becoming more lucid. The remains of my lunch were there – squashed and messy, but it was food. I ate a tiny portion, saving the rest for later. It wouldn't last long but it was something. The soup in my thermos was lukewarm but it tasted good.

I had read of climbers surviving by building a snow-hole. But I had no idea where to start, and with only one good arm it seemed an impossible task.

After about an hour slithering around on my stomach I had gouged out a hole about six inches deep and a few feet long. It was hopeless. The tears of frustration were warm on my cheeks. I ate another morsel of food and drank some more of my soup – cold.

I just can't do any more. It wouldn't protect me anyway. If it snows overnight no one will find me . . . until the spring. Joe, where are you? Why have you not sent help? What if he's dead?

All around was still and quiet. It was unbearable so I screamed – Joe's name – but it echoed back in the stillness.

A bright star was shining above me. That same star was seen by people all over the country – going home from work, going out for the evening. *Going out for the evening . . . .*

What day is it? Saturday? Sunday? If it's Sunday I should be at

84

work tomorrow. I'm so sleepy. What if I fall asleep and never wake up? What if they never find my body? Oh, Mum, what will you do? I'm sorry for the pain I'm causing you. Joe, where are you? Better keep awake.

I tried the phone again. In the dark I had to guess where the '9' was. This time it did not bleep but rang and a voice answered. *There's hope.* Then it went dead. I redialled and there was nothing. Over and over I dialled and there was nothing.

If I leave it switched on someone might get through to me. But that will waste the battery and I might need it in the morning. No. The morning probably won't come for me. Better to live for tonight.

But the phone did not ring. No one could get through – if anyone was trying.

I had come to the end of the world. I was falling off the edge. Down. Down. Down . . . . I could see lights. I could hear voices. The wolves were howling. I was finished.

A light shining in my face wakened me. A dog was barking somewhere nearby. A figure in black stood over me. I was terrified. What was going on? I was cold, very cold. I started to cry and could not stop shaking.

"You're all right, now. We've found you."

"Who are you? Where am I? What happened?"

"You're going to be all right." Another figure appeared and leaned over me. I could hear other voices.

"Bring the stretcher."

"Give her a whiff."

'My leg . . . my arm." I sobbed.

"We'll help you. You'll be all right now."

"We'll soon have you off this hill."

"What happened to Joe?"

I saw the look which passed between the two and I knew.

The blackness was closing in again.

WINTER BITES
L.A. Hollywood

Icy water trickles over a
stream bed as it curves
through the valley,
leafless trees showing their
beauty once again.

Here and there snow-laden
branches in trees creak,
crack, break with the weight
of snow, falling across the
stream or into the forest.

As winter bites
smoke drifts up from fires in
farms cut off, phones down,
roads impassable.

Carrion-seekers fly in the daylight
hours, looking for food that
may keep them going till
spring.

From the high mountains
comes the stag with his herd
to forage in the trees,
eating the coarse grass
through the winter.

THE GOLD DIGGER
Fiona Lang

L ate in the day the weather had turned. Setting aside his laptop, Iain raked at the fire, unable to shake the chill that lay about his bones. He flexed his feet inside his socks, enjoying the heat. It was proving difficult to crop Morag out of his holiday photos, not for sentimental reasons, but because her long, auburn hair had so often blown across his face in the fresh, coastal breezes of the Algarve. Finally he found one where you would never know she had existed. He also uploaded a photograph of his motorbike, and one grinning triumphantly on top of Ben Wyvis.

Poor Morag. She had taken it very well really. It hadn't been easy for him. He had hardly been able to choke down that last meal that she had cooked. After dinner he had decided that he could wait no longer. Her sparkling smile had turned to shock and confusion, and then had gone blank. Finally she had just sat there with silent tears running down her face. Why had she had to cry like that? Surely she must have known that it was coming.

That last holiday in Portugal had been the breaking point; there had been a phone call to say that her mother had been taken into hospital. When she insisted on coming home he said nothing. He just stood back and took a cold, hard look at the situation. It was always going to be this way with Morag, he realised. The boy had been taken in by a neighbour, so there would have been nothing to stop them enjoying the rest of their holiday. And then of course there had been the news that Morag's mother would be moving in with her.

Out in the darkness of the night cows charged headlong in the field, not knowing where to put themselves in their panic. Iain was unaware of their fright, but heard the gale that screamed across the roof. He was glad of the fire and his tumbler of whisky. He wished he had put the tarp over the bike, but he had been distracted, after all. His eyes went to the mantelpiece and the gold that glittered in the firelight.

Pushing back the boundary of the garden he had found a massive earth mound scattered with rabbit burrows. So that was where the little buggars had been coming from. He sent a ferret down and sat on the mound to wait, imagining the new woman that he was going to find. As he lit his cigarette, not so much as the clap of a wood pigeon's wing stirred the air. The blue-grey smoke idled and twisted, mixing with the smell of dry earth and broken stems, and hung suspended in the leafy shade as if time itself had stopped. The beasts in the field fell silent, and the darkening trees hummed and throbbed as if filled with the mutterings of another world.

Iain was oblivious as he planned his profile for the dating website. He would say that he was loyal of course; that was expected. What Morag hadn't known had never harmed her. *Good humoured, sensitive guy, genuine and honest, looking for a special lady to share good times and the finer things in life.* She would be vivacious, athletic and spontaneous; someone who enjoyed packing a bag at a moment's notice and heading off. Not too tied down. His tag line would be *'looking for a princess'.* It might be corny, but it had worked before.

Eventually he became aware that the ferret had not resurfaced, and, cursing it, he fetched a spade and began demolishing the mound. It was full of large stones so it was hard work. Even after a hot bath his bones ached, and the whisky hadn't cured him of the shivers that ran up and down his spine. Morag had always looked after him very well when he was ill, and he wished that he hadn't ended things so precipitously. He should have found his new woman first. Maybe Morag would still come if he called: if he exaggerated enough.

Taking another swig of whisky, he fumbled and missed as he set it down. The tumbler turned on its side and poured its contents onto the book that he'd been using as a coaster. He cursed, wiping splashes from the keyboard. With luck Morag would have forgotten that she had ever given it to him. He hadn't read it and didn't plan to. What did these so called experts know? Iain knew exactly what the boy needed: a kick in the pants and to be shown who was boss. Morag always had an excuse. She said that he needed careful, patient work, to not be made anxious and to be taught new skills gradually. Rubbish! That boy had her wrapped around his little finger.

One of the few times he came here, he made up a story about

seeing a green lady. Iain had been derisively tutting as he watched him flapping his arms and talking to himself alone at the bottom of the garden. So he knew it was entirely a piece of fiction; there had been nobody there. And the next time Morag brought him he wouldn't even get out of the car because he said he was too scared. It was a complete manipulation. The only reason he was scared was because he realised he had met his match. Iain didn't have children of his own, but felt this gave him a much better perspective than Morag. He couldn't abide the way people put their children at the centre of their lives. Like a dog made to sleep outside, the boy had to be shown that the world didn't begin and end with him.

If it had been up to Iain he would have taken the Pokemon or whatever rubbish it was that fascinated him and put it all straight into the bin. He would have had him outdoors in the fresh air working hard, whether he liked it or not. There would have been no more special treatment. How would he ever learn to be normal if he was allowed to sit indoors playing computer games and talking to himself?

Morag had said that she wasn't trying to make him normal! That had spoken volumes! She said that she loved and accepted her son for who he was, and that progress would come in small steps. Iain could have turned that boy around in an instant if she hadn't stood in his way. Pandering to him was doing him no favours; he should be disciplined into at least the illusion of normality, and taught some semblance of usefulness.

He put the whisky-sodden book on the fire; it was where it belonged. The flames flared up and then burned an unnatural, simmering green. You had to enter into his world, Morag had said, because he couldn't enter into ours! There was only one world that Iain knew: the cold, hard, practical world of reality. The boy had to face it.

But Morag and her burdens were not his concern anymore. He was looking only forwards, to carefree times ahead. There were enough lonely women out there for him to take his pick. If it was for the right one he might be prepared to travel some distance, within reason. And after all Morag had relocated, back when he had led her to believe that they might move in together. He had never really wanted that, though. He was comfortable as he was, and moving would have meant a lot of hard work and inconvenience. She had been fine in her little rented cottage. It would be crowded now with her mother, but he could hardly have been expected to make the sacrifice, especially when she wouldn't take his advice.

Life would be so much better with his new princess. He imagined that she would be young and slender, good salary, own home, no baggage, no children. Raking a hand through his silvery beard, he wondered how low he could set his preferred age. Morag had built up his confidence, and he thought that even 25 might not be out of the question. A thin scratching started up behind the walls. He would need to set more traps. He put 25 - what the heck! - and decided not to answer the question about income. Best not risk attracting any gold diggers. In three years, Morag had never suspected just how much money he really had.

His eyes went again to the mantel. He had never seen gold like it before; it almost seemed to glow from within. Reflected firelight swam across its surface like the glinting of a thousand malevolent eyes as Iain allowed himself to wonder whether 18 would be a possibility.

Digging into the mound, he had unearthed stone after stone, large and smooth and flat at one end. He stacked them with satisfaction; good stones could be hard to find. He whistled as he worked, but the sound didn't echo through the trees. It fell at his feet as if something unseen pressed in heavily all around him. He was too busy to notice. He was only thinking that he would use the stones to build a wall to mark the new boundary that he was creating.

When he found the hoard that lay within the mound, he forgot the stones. In the space of only minutes he pulled out celtic brooches and torcs, and most staggering of all a crown, elaborately decorated with knotwork and zoomorphic embellishments. Untouched by time, they shone with such a soft, pure light that he imagined his hands being the first to ever hold them. They wouldn't be going to any museum, that was for sure. He would excavate the mound himself, and whatever more was in it would be his. He would arrange a private sale.

The old farmer who owned the land hadn't noticed him gradually extending the boundary of his garden year by year; he was unlikely to notice the excavations. No one ever ventured into the woods. Local superstition had it to be a darkly magical place.

He sank his teeth into the last slice of Morag's fruit cake, his perfectly whitened teeth mashing through its sweet, caramelised moistness. He felt sorry for himself tonight. A strange gloom had come over him, along with the chill, as if a cold shadow had been cast. He would miss Morag's baking, and her laughter, and her crazy optimism. He had loved her, and had even imagined for a while that they would be together forever. Scanning the room morosely, he was already missing the way she tidied up after him when she came over. Poor Morag. For all her laughter, she had aged in the time he had known her, and she was always tired. Iain blamed the boy. Still, what could be done if she wouldn't take the hard line that he had suggested? Yes, it had all been a very big disappointment.

Out in the darkness, the gale subsided as quickly as it had got up and was replaced by a curious hush, like the brushing of velvet, or the creeping of small, furred bodies. A fat, white moth trembled, trapped in a spider's web. Thin fingers picked it from its bonds, and rows of small, sharp teeth chewed. And then the front door crashed open. His princess had arrived.

When Iain was found he was still in his chair. The laptop lay smashed on the hearth, and his possessions had been thrown about the room as if a whirlwind had been through them. Leaves had even been blown up against the insides of the windows. A curious collection of knotted twigs had been arranged on the mantel, along with a crown of twisted stems.

They said it was a stroke, and perhaps that was why his eyes had a strange, almost metallic glaze. If you had looked really deeply into them it would have been like sinking to the bottom of a summer pond. And if you had looked for too long you would have felt yourself slipping away from all you had ever known.

No one else ever saw the faerie gold. It was back where it belonged, earth mound and walls rebuilt as if they had never been disturbed. No trace of Iain remains. Only on certain nights of the year, near midnight, you might see the lost ferret. Whiter than ordinary white, it dances through the woods, its fur tipped with sparks, and a wild glaze in its eyes.

THE CARMEN MIRANDA HAT
Frances Abbot

The Carmen Miranda hat came out of the old trunk smelling faintly of cedar wood, but looking as fresh and vivid as the day I had put it away. Looking after my neighbour's two children was rather tiring and I was beginning to regret my offer when I struck on the idea of dressing up, a great favourite from my own childhood and, though they were initially unenthusiastic, obviously not at all used to the idea, they good-naturedly helped drag the trunk from the cupboard under the stairs.

Lifting the lid was like lifting the lid on my past. My parents had both been actors on the amateur stage and they had kept some of the costumes and props they used. As an only child I had often spent long afternoons in an imaginary world fuelled by feather boas, fans and mutton-sleeved dresses. I could be a villain with the aid of a long black cloak, top hat and silver-topped cane, or a king in a cardboard crown stuck with coloured glass jewels and rimmed with cotton wool fur. I could be anything I wanted with a little bit of imagination and a few appropriate props.

The two children were not quite sure how to react to the parasols and satin shoes which were first to be lifted from the tissue paper, but underneath was a selection of pantomime wigs and a pair of slap-me-thigh boots. From that point I didn't have to do anything. I sat back in my rocker and watched. It turns out that children haven't changed all that much over the years. They swaggered and primped in front of the mirror much as I had done all those years ago, thrust and parried with wooden swords and died lingering deaths on the carpet.

I, meanwhile, had found the Carmen Miranda hat. Alone out of the contents of the trunk this did not belong to Father or Mother. This belonged to me. It belonged to a period of austerity, of make do and mend, of bombings and air raids and our boys home on leave and the brief period when I no longer felt alone. I had someone of my own who loved me. We met at a party. It was to be fancy dress, cocking a snoot at rationing and shortages. Father and Mother had the dressing up box to rely on, but I fashioned my costume myself. The clothes were easily done. They just had to be colourful and flamboyant. The hat was a different matter, but I was proud of the result, a multi-coloured beehive of a turban with artificial fruit strongly glued to the front.

To this day I don't know what I was thinking when choosing to portray such a showy character. I did not have any of my parents' theatrical flair, just the opposite. I don't say I lived in their shadow. They were far too well-meaning and caring of me to deliberately put me in the shade. But still, I seemed all the more timid in comparison to their confident conviviality. So there we were, Sweeney Todd, Queen Mab and Carmen Miranda. Pete told me later that he saw us the moment we entered the room. He couldn't tell who the other two characters were, but he knew mine straight away. I saw him when he danced up to me where I sat, using his arms and swaying his hips in the rhythm of the Latin style. He was smiling broadly and it was impossible not to smile back.

He was a flashy GI Joe and I was the epitome of middle-class English reserve. Our speedy courtship and engagement surprised everyone, but my parents were drawn to him as much as I was and they made no objection. I suspect they were relieved to find that I was marriageable after all. But I didn't get married. Pete was reported missing in action six weeks before VE day. I packed away my future when I laid that hat in the trunk and resigned myself to what I eventually became, what I am today.

My neighbour returned for her two older children while they were still engrossed in the contents of the trunk, her youngest, no longer blue from a coughing fit, snugly asleep in the mother's arms. She was still ruffled from the dash to the hospital and I made her sit while I brewed us a pot of tea. I can't move around well these days so by the time I wheeled the trolley in she had had time to relax into the big cushions of the armchair. She seemed almost as drowsy as the baby. The older children appeared to catch her mood and they sat contentedly at her feet examining their finds. We sat in companionable silence until she set down her cup and straightened her back. She reached out to pick up the hat which I had left on the table.

I did not know this woman although she had been living next door for the past year. I do not get out much now and when I did, before the arthritis became so severe, I always kept very much to myself. She had only come to my door in the direst emergency. So I surprised myself as much as her when I began to tell her about Carmen Miranda and the war days and Pete. She was a good listener and I sensed empathy rather than sympathy while I talked.

She held the hat out to me when I had come to a stop.

"Would you like to put it on?" she asked.

Being careful not to wake him, she placed the baby on her vacant chair and with equal gentleness put the bright beehive on my head. I could feel her tucking in the tendrils of my wispy hair and I had a sudden flashback of myself doing the same thing those many years ago when my hair was strong and black. Satisfied, she crossed the room and brought me from her large bag a good-sized hand mirror, then stood back while I looked at myself. Under the gaudy colours and the imperfect imitations of bananas and pears was framed a face of paper-thin skin raddled with deeply scored lines and wrinkles. I looked from the travesty in the mirror to the domestic scene in front of me and I felt the beginning of tears.

"JUST IN CASE . . ."
Christina Macdonald

Hurry up Kirsty-Anne. Eat your toast quickly!"
Morag was hopping up and down outside her friend's gate, her new bicycle propped up carefully against the fence.

Kirsty-Anne gave a nonchalant wave and disappeared into her garden shed. After a lot of banging and thumping she emerged wheeling out her new acquisition.

Morag eyed it with the tiniest feeling of jealousy. This one had chrome wheels – hers were black but she'd got hers before Kirsty. The plain ones came sooner.

Dad had sent away for it and she'd had it for two weeks. They'd cycled round the town and gone down to the boat last Saturday night, but today was going to be exciting. They were cycling, just the two of them – no grown-ups – down to the Cockle Ebb.

"Hurry up, Kirsty, the sun's getting hotter. I'm dying to go to the beach."

Kirsty wheeled her bike down the side path. Morag lifted the gate latch for her and they stood together on the pavement.

"Which way will we go?"

"It'll be shorter if we go up the brae and cut across," said Kirsty confidently. She was a year older than Morag and wiser in her own eyes.

The July sun was high in the sky and the slight breeze behind them filled them with energy.

"Kirsty, go slower. I can't keep up!" Morag panted, pedalling up the steep hill, her ginger curls bobbing in the wind. Kirsty was pedalling strongly in front, her long black hair waving behind her, just like a mermaid, Morag thought wistfully.

"I'll wait for you at the top."

When Morag reached the top Kirsty was sitting on the bus stop seat. "You took your time!"

The run down the hill on the other side was fun. They tried to cycle together but Kirsty said her Dad said you shouldn't cycle together on the roads in case a car came.

At the bottom of the brae stood an old farmhouse. From there a bumpy rutted track ran down to the Cockle Ebb. They careered down, screaming and yelling avoiding the pot-holes and the watery rush-grown ditches, past the well where Morag's Dad had filled the cans when the water was off and there in front of them lay the perfect picnic place. Beyond them stretched a blue sea that seemed to go on forever and golden sand strewn with cockle shells.

Pushing their bikes over the sandy hollows, through the spiky grass, they searched for a sheltered place. That was one of the best things about this beach – there were lots of little places where you could hide.

The machair was a gem-studded field of flowers. Morag loved this place where pink and white clover, yellow vetch and sea pinks all jostled together for space on the grass.

She sat down to take off her socks and sandals. There was a lovely smell of honey in the air. Small brown bees were bumbling their way from flower to flower. Morag turned over and lay on her back for a while, drinking in the freshness of the sea air and the blueness of the sky. It was a perfect bit of peace after the noisiness of the others she'd left behind.

Kirsty had already stripped off down to her red woollen costume. She'd strewn her clothes all round in her excitement, her vest and knickers clinging to the grasses like little flags.

Morag peeled off her skirt and jumper and the cardigan Auntie had made her wear "just in case!" Just in case of what? Morag wondered. Auntie had knitted her cozzie, a dark blue it was. It was getting tight. She was conscious of her two little budding breasts. Kirsty's were a bit bigger she'd noticed, but then she was a year older after all.

Morag dumped her clothes in a heap and raced down over the sand to join Kirsty, the sand soft at first and then firm beneath her toes as she neared the water. Yelping and hopping as the shells grazed her bare feet, she threw herself into the water. "Ooooh!" How could the sun be so warm and the sea so cold?

By now they could see other groups of children spread out along the wide curved beach, screaming and laughing as they galloped in and out of the sea.

When they'd exhausted themselves dodging the incoming waves Kirsty and Morag knelt near the water's edge and built a castle with a moat.

"Put this gull's feather on top for a flag." They sat back and watched the tide invade their work of art. "Let's guess how long before the sea gets it."

They waded up through the dunes to their little hollow, sat down on their towels and opened up their sandwiches.

"Oh, you've got Spam in yours!" Morag eyed Kirsty's packet.

"Gis one of yours and I'll give you an egg one."

Kirsty handed over the desired sandwich and looked disdainfully at Morag's offering.

"Does your Auntie ever make any other kind?" Morag blushed.

"Well, it's because we've hens that she makes them." She wasn't going to say that they couldn't afford much else to put in them – not just now when Dad was out of work again.

Kirsty had a bottle of lemonade she'd got with the shopping from the corner shop down town. She took a swig and offered it graciously to Morag.

"My Auntie says you shouldn't put your mouth to someone else's bottle," and she unscrewed her own. Kirsty fancied the orange juice but said nothing. Morag delved into the bottom of her basket.

"Hurray! Auntie's put in something else! I've found some sweeties." She held out four toffees in crinkly paper.

"Mrs Macdonald brought us some the other day. She got them with her sweetie coupons and Auntie put them away on the top shelf, just in case."

"Just in case of what?" enquired Kirsty.

"Just in case we ate them all at once, I suppose."

"Share them out!"

Morag felt very important.

"Yes, you can have two if you give me back two when YOU get

some." They nodded in agreement and sat in silence for a few moments savouring the sweetness and chewyness of the unexpected treat.

The sun had gone behind a cloud and a chilly wind was beginning to blow off the sea.

"We'd better get dressed now. Mam said not to be late."

Kirsty stood up and went to round up her clothes. She gave a loud shriek.

"Look what's happened to my vest!" Kirsty was holding up her white vest which was now green and full of holes round the bottom.

Morag rushed to find her own clothes and promptly burst into tears.

"Oh, Kirsty, look at mine too!"

There, clinging to some spiky grass a few feet away was HER vest. Hers was green and holey too but it was the straps on hers that had vanished. Kirsty began to laugh hysterically.

"I know what's done it!" she shouted, pointing at the culprit – a large brown cow contentedly chewing the cud a few yards away. "It must have thought it was a new treat!"

"Anyway, I don't care! I'm going to wear mine home." With that she stripped off her costume, dried herself, slipping the holey vest over her head followed by the rest of her clothes.

Morag started to bubble again.

"I can't wear mine 'cos the top's all eaten and it's all sticky and horrible. I'm scared. Auntie's going to give me an awful row. I just know it!"

She rubbed the sand off with her towel and began to dress minus the vest. She folded the bedraggled garment carefully, trying not to touch the sticky green mess.

"I'll put in the bottom of the basket so's Auntie won't notice –for a while anyway!"

They faced into the wind on the way home. She was glad Auntie had told her to take her cardigan – just in case – though she doubted Auntie had meant "just in case a cow eats your vest!"

MEETING D
L.A. Hollywood

She sits in the back of the church holding a bent ring. It looks out of place in the leather-gloved hand; four thin bands, two gold, two silver, intertwined. She only half hears the words spoken by some preacher about people and things he knows nothing about, before they lay the coffin in the ground to be forgotten with time. While the preacher makes the sign of the cross and says a prayer for the drunk who did this to her family, D leaves to sit on her bike, wrap a piece of denim round the ring, put it in a box and slip it into an inside pocket of her cut-down jeans. Then, on the roaring bike, face to the wind, she heads for the hospital where she spins to a stop in the car park.

Going through the doors, her boots ring out with each step she takes down the passageway. They knew she would come. Lady D goes into the room where three women sit round a bed. In the bed a woman lies with tubes going into her. Next to the bed, in a glass box, is a baby. More tubes. D moves to the woman, removes a strand of hair from her face, then bends to kiss her forehead with more tenderness than anyone had ever seen from her.

She looks at the three women for the first time and hands one a bag full of money. "Stay with her. If you need more call the banker. I'm gone." Her boots echo back down the passageway. People move out of her way. Those that knew her knew she would come today. She thunders out of the car park. Tonight some drunk driver will meet the reaper head-on with a little help from Lady D.

STORM MAD
Jim Piper

John, come up and say goodnight to the children." "Hang on, Sally, I'm watching the last of this survival show - it has just about finished."

"John, it's twenty to eight and they have school tomorrow and anyway you're videoing it."

John said goodnight while Sally tucked them in.

"Goodnight, Annie. Goodnight, Joe; sleep tight and mind the bugs don't bite."

"Goodnight, Dad."

John hurried back down stairs to catch the last of the show about building a shelter of sticks, leaves and moss. As Sally came into the lounge a severe weather warning was flashed up on the screen.

"It's brewing up a storm out there," said John. "They're forecasting gusts up to ninety mile an hour after midnight."

"It's a good job we are all safe and warm in here," she replied.

"I think I'll go out there and see what it's like."

"Are you completely mad, John Taylor? Please tell me you are joking. It is already really rough out there."

"Sally, nobody's got any sense of adventure these days. Take my great great-uncle Joshua. He was the ship's mate, on a huge sailing vessel clipper. They weathered a hurricane out at sea, sixty foot plus waves and he never lost one crew member."

"No, John, but you've lost your marbles and it's a mad idea."

"Well, I'm just going out there to see what happens to all the birds and animals. After a hurricane you don't see piles of dead birds and other animals do you?" John sat back to watch the next programme.

Sally went off muttering, "The man's mad, mad! Lost it completely, he's having a mid life crisis."

The phone rang, and Sally answered it. "Hello, Jenny. Yes, we're fine just now. Yes, we have candles and torches. Thanks for ringing. See you tomorrow for coffee if the storm stops." Sally came into the lounge.

"That was Jenny."

"Yes, I heard."

"John, she's really nice. We are so lucky to have them as neighbours."

"I've seen her, Sal, in the Jeep, probably spends all day in that big new house, polishing her nails and home shopping on the internet."

"Keep your voice down. The children will hear you. You don't want it to get repeated. Jenny is very nice, so is Anthony, her husband." She went off in a huff.

At eleven o'clock John called out, "Right, that's it, Sal. I'm off."

"What do you think you are doing, a married man with two young school children and responsibilities."

"I'm going out and that is it. I'll be fine. I know how to dodge about out there."

"Well, John Taylor. You will be sleeping on the sofa when and if you get home, and just for one night if you're lucky." She hurried off to the kitchen.

John put on his hiking gear, grabbed his fishing hip flask from its hideaway and headed out the door, down the garden, and through the back gate, out into the fields. The wind nearly knocked him off his feet. The moon was just out from behind the racing clouds, illuminating, on his left, the tall pines that bowed in the wind like a row of monks. To his right, a hundred yards away, stood the old field boundary wall. He edged towards it. A plastic lid flew past his head going down the valley. *Whew that was close!* Seconds later one of the pines fell, broken like snapping a match. John faced into the west wind, bent down, humbled by the power of nature, and headed diagonally west towards the stone wall.

His plan was to move down the leeward side of it out of the storm. Before reaching it a small branch hit him fully amidships. Flinching, he doubled his efforts to reach the wall. *Nearly there*, he thought. Something inside him, some kind of sixth sense, made him hit the ground as at that moment the remnants of a poly tunnel, travelling at speed, glanced off his back taking his breath away. He stood up and managed to reach a corner in the wall, shaken and trembling. He sat down behind it, rubbing his wounds. Looked around he took out his hip flask and took a large draught, the metal rattling against his teeth. There were no signs of any birds or animals.

"This is really wild crazy, but I can't go back now. What will Sally think of me? She will probably rub it in. He pulled his woolly hat down over his ears and his parka hood over that and tucked in against the old wall for security. The shaking was slowing down as he took some more brandy.

His thoughts went forward to the next day, Wednesday, signing on. There was with no job on the horizon since the filling station had closed down three months ago. Available jobs seemed to be getting less. Every week Kirsty at the Job Centre asked him politely with a smile.

"Have you been looking for work?"

"Yes, of course," he'd say. John drifted off into a day dream despite the noise and aching shoulders.

He was on his way in the car, in the storm, just entering town. As he drew nearer, with the wind blowing hard and the trees bending, he noticed the bus shelter near the Job Centre blown over.

He slowed down; shop signs were bouncing off his car. He came to a halt. He got out of the car and bending against the wind made for the shelter. He peered underneath; it was Kirsty.

"Mr Taylor, the Job Centre sent me home. I've been trapped under here for an hour." John looked around hastily. Not far away was a large broken fencepost. He picked it up, pushed it under the shelter and with a wild adrenalin-fuelled heave managed to lift the shelter up a foot or so.

"Kirsty, get out quick," he shouted. "Get out fast." She just made it as his grip gave - just before the shelter crumpled to the ground.

At that moment he was awakened from his dream by a sickening, twisting noise followed by a crashing sound. He opened his eyes and staggered to his feet. By the moon's light he could just make out the rowan tree on the west of their cottage leaning against the roof on the children's bedroom.

"Oh dear God! Sally and the kids." The tree was being moved

about by the wind; slates were smashing to the ground. With legs of lead and by torch light he headed for home. All the house lights round about had gone out - a power cut. His heart pounded in his chest cavity. Pushed behind by the wind, he made it to the back gate. Inside the garden and, with fading torch light, he tripped over some bushes and landed flat on his face in the cabbage patch. Frantically he regained his feet and got to the back door. Fumbling for his keys, and with dirty hands, he entered the cottage.

"Sally, Joe, Annie." He shouted. There was no reply. He raced up the stairs, muddy boots and all. The children's bedroom door was jammed due to the tree pushing on the roof. He opened the other bedroom door; no Sally. Racing back down into the kitchen he saw the note on the table.

"Worried about storm and you. We have gone to Jenny's. Midnight. Love Sally."

John took stock of the situation. There he was, covered in mud, having gone out in a storm and left his wife and young children. He took off his parka, rolled it up and left it in the hallway. By candle light he went upstairs and changed his trousers. The wind was dying down outside as he wiped his face with a towel. Putting clean shoes on, he headed off to Anthony and Jenny's house. He had never felt so ashamed of himself. Climbing over a fallen tree and with a little help from the moon he reached the house, wondering if he was actually in a nightmare. No; a hard pinch proved he was awake. As he drew nearer he could just make out a face at the window. It was Sally's. She opened the front door and came out to meet him. John braced himself for a tirade. Instead she hugged him, taking all the wind from his sails.

"John, thank God you're back." Once inside the children hugged him too.

"Anthony, thank you so much for taking in my family. You are so kind."

"Would you like a dram?" Anthony came over.

"No thanks, Anthony. A cup of tea would be nice."

"Dad, how was it out there?" What could he say?

"It was wild but I survived."

"Gosh, Dad, you're really brave."

Sally whispered in his ear, "We've got the spare double room. The kids have their own. Tony says we can stay here for a while until we get sorted out." Deep, deep inside, John felt an overwhelming guilt in the pit of his stomach.

"Can I use the toilet, Tony?"

"Yes, it's up the stairs to the right. Jenny's upstairs in her office doing some work on her laptop. It runs on battery power." At that moment the lights came back on. A cheer went up.

Upstairs, Jenny came out of her home office as John was leaving the bathroom where he had been sick.

"Hello, John, I see you're OK now."

"Yes."

"Sally was deeply worried about you."

John tried to change the subject.

"Nice little office you have there, Jenny."

"Come in and have a look. There's a really good view from this little window here. Sally would be amazed. You can see most of the big old stone wall."

John gulped; she knew how he had really faced the storm.

"I was up here finishing some urgent work during the height of the storm. Sally says you went out into the storm to prove you are a man."

"Sort of. It's not easy being unemployed with no work around, you know."

"Well, John, don't worry. I can keep a secret. That's when I am not polishing my nails and home shopping." John felt his face turning red. Another secret out.

"The storm has done a lot of damage to our garden. Sally tells me when you two first met, that you worked for a gardening company. My work involves helping people to start up new businesses. I could help you. How about starting up your own garden business?"

"Sounds good to me."

"And, John, Sally would really like to go to her mother's near Blackpool for a holiday this year, not wilderness camping in Wales."

"Thank you, Jenny. It looks like *you're* the hero now."

BLACK BOB
Fiona Lang

He came in a cart pulled by two black dogs. Whether they could not or would not cross the boundary, I don't know. He stood just beyond the gate, though it was open, and he carried a rattle of moth cocoons and seal whiskers. He was no ordinary tinker.

"What ails you, old man?" he asked. As he spoke his lips moved, but the words seemed to come instead from the rattle as he shook it. His voice was like bones cracking.

"Nothing ails me but age," I immediately replied. There was no deal to be made here; no barter that I wished to enter into.

"And are you more afraid of dying, or of living?" he asked, leering at me with one amber eye from behind a curtain of greasy hair. I wondered how much was question, and how much was threat. The black feathers of his cloak stirred strangely.

"I'm not afraid of either," I lied, standing my ground.

"For how much longer do you think you can walk that mile to town and back?"

"I can do it for as long as is needed."

"When you climb alone into your bed at night, old man, do you ache against the hard mattress, feeling that you have climbed into a sea of pain?"

"There's no remedy for age," but I wondered if he did have a remedy for sale in the fish skin pouch that he held. I would buy it if it would make him go away.

"The question is, are you strong enough to face another winter?" His voice was softer now, hissing, like sleet.

"I am indeed," I answered proudly, though I was not. I had reached the end of my strength some time since. His dogs cowered, with pleading eyes, in the silence that followed.

"Give me water from that pump there, and things will go easier for you."

Believing this to be a threat, I motioned with shaking hands for him to pass. Amongst the raven's feathers, his cloak was hung with dew claws and beaks. He smelt of dry earth, and crackled like withered stalks.

He passed out of sight around the house, and I heard water flowing from the old pump, though it had seized up many years ago; I had been afraid to tell him. The sound was unearthly in the still air; a deep burbling, like strange and lively voices in conversation.

The day stood silent and white. As I waited, a thin drift of smoke from the fire was all that moved. Wan brown against the pressing fog, it crept from the chimney before melting away. Every living thing was made dark and earth-bound by the damp and chill.

Overcome by dread, I was unable to look towards the dogs beyond the gate. Somehow I knew that they were not dogs at all but men transformed, crouching on all fours. I could not bring myself to see them.

The water fell silent but he did not return, and when I dared to look he had vanished. There was no sign of him, though I clearly heard wheels and the padding of paws.

True to his word things have gone easier since that day. My fire throws out a generous heat that warms me through. Friends and neighbours who once had no thought of me have taken to visiting. Most of all, when I climb into my bed at night I find only comfort in the mattress, and not pain.

Still, there is dread in this good fortune, and a fear that my visitor may return. Was he angel or devil? Or both?

On days when I wake to find the world once again cold and wrapped in cloud, I sit indoors alone, too afraid to venture out. I don't understand what bargain it was that I made. Two local men didn't return home that day; their fishing boat was lost. If he comes again, you see, I fear it may be my turn to draw the cart.

JUST GETTING DRUNK
L.A. Hollywood

Linda sits there thinking about the night so long ago when she sat in the hall not being able to dance like her friends.

She drank with eyes closed, just letting the sounds move her inside from what she thinks she is. Suddenly the drinking stopped as a chair moved and a shadow fell across the table. A hand took her drink away as she slumped in her chair, out cold.

Someone took her home, put her to bed, and then sat by the window to doze till six in the morning when he slipped out to buy her ten red roses, all long stemmed. Back in Linda's flat Nelson found a vase and putting the flowers in it left a note.

DON'T TRY SO HARD NEXT TIME. BACK AT SEVEN.

Linda woke to a throbbing head and a mouth that felt like a dead cat had been dragged through it backwards. With a screaming bladder she groaned her way to the bathroom without looking in the mirror; she'd seen it all before. Slumping in her chair she headed for the kitchen, made coffee, lit a fag, looked at the note, and then down at her nightdress, finding buttons done up wrong. She dropped the fag in the sink and headed for the shower as a growling came from inside her for food. Dressed, she went to the corner shop for her weekly things without too much hope of seeing anyone.

That evening was the start of it all. After that, a year of long friendship, a second to become soul mates and this year he's there kneeling beside her in a church slipping a ring on her finger. Nelson moves behind Linda. She leans back in her chair. He takes the handles and pushes her down the aisle of the church to a new life as his wife.

A PRAYER FOR VALENTINE'S DAY
Christina Macdonald

Let there be no roses on my table,
No promises on this Saint's Day.
Shed no secret tears for that emotion
Which died along Life's way.

Let there be no roses on my pillow
Their fragrant beauty in memory retain
But when perhaps you lie alone and lonely
May sweet slumber ease away your pain.

Let there be no roses by my grave-stone
Red roses speak of love, white roses peace,
But when at last you come, perhaps, to mourn me
May these sweet blessings bring your heart release.

LOON LAKE
Louise James

Ruth had begged Mum to let us row across Loon Lake. She was my big sister and very persistent. I didn't really want to go but her dominance over me was complete and I mouthed agreement. We set off from the rickety dock, Ruth, naturally, at the oars for she was strong, and me, trailing a hand in the still water, feigning nonchalance. Swish, swish went the slightly erratic oars but I was soon distracted by a dark object several feet below the surface, waving like seaweed but this wasn't weed, and it came back to me that Bobby Mackie had drowned in Loon Lake the summer I was seven. My eyes followed the shape as it floated along behind us, losing distance as Ruth rowed steadily on. I knew Bobby and we used to play on the dock, that summer. I might have been the last person to see him; I 'm not sure; I can't really remember.

After a while we reached the dock outside Taylors' cabin; Ruth bumped us up to the old tire and grabbed hold. She knew better than to ask me to tie on, for that would mean standing up and clambering over the seats, which we had always been told not to do. Instead she made the necessary manoeuvres herself, recovering quickly when she leaned over too far at the first attempt.

Kenny Taylor appeared on the dock and helped us up. He was fifteen or sixteen and had terrible acne but was always nice; I liked him but Ruth didn't. She said he always took over the rod when they went fishing with our dads and there was a big one on the line. I knew that she'd dropped his new rod and reel overboard two summers ago but didn't say. Kenny was going to row us back because Mrs Taylor was worried about the sky.

After milk and cookies, we got ready to go. Ruth was unhappy with the new arrangements and plonked herself down in the stern with a scowl while I took up my position in the bow. Again I leaned over the gunnels, unable to take my eyes off the water as we headed towards the far shore.

A mid-afternoon squall caught Kenny off guard and spun the tiny boat around; I could see by her face that Ruth was relieved she wasn't rowing but then she looked worried and shouted for me to 'sit low'. But it was too late; another gust swung the boat round again and I fell overboard. I bobbed up with spluttering yelps hoping that Ruth – and more helpfully, Kenny, had seen my dilemma. But while struggling to tread water and reach for the outstretched oar, I was petrified to feel something dragging me under by the legs. I felt soft fabric and saw what seemed to be a jacket, just like the one Bobby had been wearing. By the time Kenny had grabbed me under the armpits and dumped me in a heap at Ruth's feet, I was screaming in terror. She let out a sob of relief as she hugged me with down-stretched arms, sinking to her knees into the sloshing wet of the boat's floor. Kenny steadied the boat and pulled strongly onwards; he was a natural boatman and I could see that he was cursing himself for losing control. After a few minutes our dock was in sight and Ruth said maybe we shouldn't tell the grownups since everything had come out OK in the end. I was still caught up in my terrors and silently nodded agreement.

As we lay in our bunks that night, I asked Ruth to tell me about the day Bobby died. At first she pretended to be asleep; then sighed, and suddenly her head appeared hanging down from the top bunk, hair spread out in spikes and drooping upside-down face.

She said it was a tragic accident and I shouldn't think about it but I started to cry. She climbed down and sat beside me, holding me awkwardly and sounding like our mother as she explained again that Bobby was epileptic and should *never* have been allowed to spend the week at the cabin with the Oberskis. Everyone knew his fits were not well controlled; it wasn't fair on others. She forgot to mention about Bobby sometimes not taking his pills and pretending he had, until I reminded her, between sobs.

At last she got to the bit where I pushed Bobby off the dock into the water, which was three feet deep, and how Pat Oberski fetched him out immediately and revived him, leaving his jacket to float away in the commotion. I ran alongside her as she carried him coughing up to the cabin and dropped him on the sofa in the sun porch.

When Pat turned to get more towels, Bobby stuck his tongue out at me and whispered that 'I'd drownded him' but no one heard but me. Then that night he choked on his tongue when he was supposed to be sleeping, and died.

Now, said Ruth, in the way of big sisters who adopt an adult manner of speaking, what are we going to do with you and that runaway imagination? This was the bit I liked best, for then she cosied down under the eiderdown beside me, rocking me gently and smoothing my hair. Before long she was fast asleep. Safe and reassured, I lay awake for quite a while, thinking about that summer, and wondering if I would ever tell about the pills I threw away when we were playing in Oberskis' cabin that morning.

TOUCHED BY CHRISTMAS
L.A. Hollywood

Bodies unseen under a piece of ship's sail that covers their bed of paper and cardboard wedged behind a gate of an abandoned office block.

Sarah breast-feeds as day breaks.

Winds blow. Decorations swing on cables across empty streets. Their lights give off eerie patterns on dead windows.

A drunk throws up, still trying to sing carols while rolling away.

Sarah looks down with tears on her face. She sees a twenty-pound note blow through the gate. With a choking in her soft voice she whispers, "Happy Christmas, Mary," and heads for the Salvation Army Hall.

JACK IN A BOX
June Munro

She sat on the terrace of The Parador overlooking the Bay of Malaga, a glass of Rioja in her hand. The warm May evening enveloped her in a medley of sounds and scents and she felt wonderfully, gloriously alive and certain of herself.

In the bay below two cruise ships lay at anchor looking down majestically and a little patronisingly at the ferry bound for Cuerta and the numerous fishing boats whose skippers were determined to maintain their place in this ancient Andalucian port. In the distance she could see a couple of private yachts, 'Gin Palaces' Jack had called them with more envy than humour in his voice as he said it. Beth smiled at the memory . . . she was free of all that now. No more listening as to how Jack would have been a millionaire now if Tom, Dick or Harry hadn't done this or not done that to him. No more pretending that his stories were new, funny or even accurate. No more smiling politely and pretending to be interested in the people Jack met in the bar or at the garage or any other place he gravitated to on his travels in the town whilst she was at home caring for Madge, his cantankerous old cow of a mother.

She shuddered slightly at the memory. How did she manage to put up with things for so long? She drained the glass of Paternina Reserva and signalled to the waiter to refill it.

"I must have been mad," she said to herself. "All those wasted years." They say it only takes one little thing, the straw that breaks the camel's back, and Beth knew that to be so true.

The day had started as usual, Jack and his mother only getting up after they heard Beth moving around in the kitchen. The three of them had moved to Spain after Jack had been made redundant and, being an only child who had been spoilt and indulged all his life, he didn't bother to ask what Beth thought of the situation. No, he had gone to see his mother who had agreed to sell her house and buy a villa with Jack – still no mention of Beth, in the hills above Granada.

The villa was part of an urbanisation of similar properties built round a communal pool, with a bar, a small supermarket and populated with the usual driftwood of humanity that can be found in any warm climate where rules are made to be broken and the local police like a quiet life. Beth had never taken to the limbo-like existence they had started to lead, the friendships that were based on the simple expedient of speaking the same language as someone, and having to accept the individual's own account of themselves. Some neighbours had disappeared at very short notice, never to be seen again and the villas they had claimed to own had been re-let or sold by agents owed money by 'Joe and Betty' or 'Inga and Hans'. On one occasion there had been a bit of a pantomime when a strange woman had appeared one evening, banging on the gates of the Villa opposite Jack and Beth's house demanding to be let in by a very embarrassed-looking 'George'. The next day 'Norma' had been seen leaving in a taxi with an assortment of cases and an irate voice screaming at her, "Leave my bloody husband alone." 'George' left a week or so later after the whole neighbourhood had been informed by the newcomer that 'Norma' was his secretary who had been having an affair with 'George' for years. They had both finally upped and left their partners and thought they had started a new life. Jack loved all the trivia and shallowness of their new life and, if Jack was happy, his mother was ecstatic, having her little boy under the same roof, and well, Beth was quiet and didn't say much, so she could be put up with too.

The three of them were sitting on the patio after lunch when Jack opined that the shepherd's pie they had had for lunch was nearly as good as his mother used to make. The smirk on his mother's face as she looked triumphantly at Beth was the last straw . . . . Beth went into the kitchen and saw the boning knife on the table beckoning her. In less than a moment she was back on the patio, standing behind Jack. Her left hand catching his head, her right hand brought the knife across the front of his throat, severing his neck from ear to ear. Before Madge could utter a word Beth was in front of her, left hand grabbing the old woman's hair and right hand again slicing across her throat. The face registered surprise – no smirk now.

Calmly, Beth spent the rest of the afternoon cleaning up the patio and placing first Jack and then Madge into two packing cases that had sat in the garage since they had moved in. The next day she had loaded Jack in his box into the boot of the car and driven towards Cartama and the construction site for the new AVE fast train service to Cordoba. She found the site foreman and with tears in her eyes explained that she had the body of an old donkey in a box and, knowing the old tradition of burying an animal in a new building, she wondered if old Jacko could perform one last task at the end of a useful life. The foreman was touched, helped her place the box on the first level of concrete and allowed her to watch the next layer being laid, submerging the box under three metres of super-strength ballast. The twenty euro note she gave him was a bonus to the glow of satisfaction he felt at helping this grieving lady.

The next day and a few miles further up the valley, the deputy foreman was similarly touched and co-operative when Beth asked if her old bitch could do one last service to the humans she had given so much pleasure to. The twenty euro note would be their little secret and the foreman need never know. She smiled as the layer of concrete covered Madge for ever.

The following weeks had been a frenzy of packing up, selling the house and explaining to anyone who asked that Jack and Madge had gone back to England having tired of life in the sun. Nobody asked too many questions; superficial relationships have their advantages.

As Beth drained her glass, she fingered the plane ticket for Australia in her handbag. A new life, maybe a new man, who knows? she mused. Just as long he isn't called Jack with a mother in tow.

116

STRUMMING
Catriona Tawse

Those hurting words which cannot be unsaid
Will stay with you
Till the ending of your days.

Alexa stands with head bowed, clasping the microphone. A cascade of black hair curtains her face. Ludo's wailing harmonica brings the number to its spine-shivering conclusion. There is a moment of silence before the crowd goes wild. People at the front get up, clapping, whistling. Soon everyone is standing. The floor resounds with the pounding of feet. Alexa leads the band off - stage to the right. She leaves her guitar on its stand. They know they will be cheered back; it is all part of the ritual. The final encore 'High Winds of Winter' has a chorus that will rock the roof. Alexa feels that rising burst of adrenalin-driven excitement. They cannot be choosy just now but their sights are set on finer things. Elegant hotels with every luxury and a uniformed welcome instead of the bored responses of motel staff warning that bills must be paid upfront.

A letter has arrived recently which Alexa at first ignores, knowing it is from her mother Kate back in Scotland in the dead-end rain-soaked west coast village of her young years. The letters have grown less pleading, less accusing, less maternal over the years. She never replies. Alexa glances through the litany of events that prompt no spark of interest.

"The new Village Hall is open at last and plans are already in hand for the 2009 celebrations, everyone is very excited."

"Big Deal," mouths Alexa.

"A leak in the upstairs bathroom almost brought down the kitchen ceiling. We were lucky that Jackie Norman the plumber came as soon as we phoned. A family of Jamaicans moved in to the old Mill House, friendly people and very musical by all accounts. Their two children are settling in well at the school. Your father is just the same as ever, there will be no getting better." She hopes that Alexa is well and still finding work and they send their love. There is no mention of Alicky.

Alicky comes lumbering in, his hair pushed up in spikes, his innocent face blotchy, twin stalactites of snot suspended from his nose. Down goes his bag with a thump and he rips the Velcro strips of his trainers. Kate wonders what the trouble is this time. She pulls some tissues from the box and calls to Marian to mind the shop a minute. She will come through if anyone needs the Post Office. Alicky tells of the wonderful sunset picture he had painted and the ruination of it when Johnny Beag knocked over a glass of water. He meant to do it, he scowls, more tears welling up. Kate hugs him and tells him Miss MacAndrew will let him do another one on Wednesday when he goes back. He brightens up and reaches for the bag to take out a jam-jar, its metal lid pierced with a few holes. Inside it a plump gold and black caterpillar is making a vain attempt to scale the smooth side. There is a tiny bit of green leaf added for its nourishment. Kate admires it and says she will put it on the high shelf for safe-keeping. Later it will be set free to go about its lawful business. All will be forgotten by morning. She asks if they have been singing today. The little group at the Special Needs unit is being patiently rehearsed in their contribution to next year's Homecoming programme.

Alicky smiles and nods, he has a great love of music. Someone from the village gave him a guitar they no longer wanted. It is his pride and joy. He sits contented for long spells on his bed strumming the thick wire strings with his fingers. It does not matter that the sound is tinny and discordant. His favourite song is 'My Bonnie Lies Over the Ocean'. Only he always sings 'flies.' Then he starts on 'Three Blind Mice'. Over and over. Often Kate wants him to stop. She sighs and leaves him be. John Alec her husband is almost deaf anyway. He was for many years the local postman, a familiar figure, dedicated and dependable. Only when his memory started to go was he relieved of his job. It did not do that certain items were delivered into the wrong hands. Soon he will come in from his work at Seòras Ruadh's garage where he cleans the buses and brushes the yard. Kate will enquire about his day. The answer will always be the same. Poor man, he is very uncomplaining. When he asks if there is news of their daughter over in America Kate will say Alexandra is fine and getting on with her life. After all this time of silence she wishes she knew if this was true.

It's 1995 and Alexa is adamant about leaving. She is almost nineteen and wants to see the world. It will be for the best. She is stifling here in this narrow minded place. They will get by without her unwilling help behind the shop counter. Her parents are bereft, confused, they implore her not to go, remind her of responsibilities. Alexa does not hear their despair, their disbelief. Tickets for the flights to the States are already bought, nothing was mentioned. All she takes is a backpack and her guitar in its case. The farewells are brief and unemotional; there is a rock where her heart should be. Her friend Donna will be at Glasgow Airport. It is a small comfort to Kate to know she will not be alone in a strange country.

There is no easy path to fame for Alexa. It is a question of survival, serving up in fast food cafes, scraping off dirty dishes, checking out cloakroom tickets. Years go by. There are no big neon signs lighting up with her name. Now she is on her own. Donna has left the poky apartment, she's gone off with a trucker. A notice in a kiosk invites would-be singers to try out at Lavelles All Night Bar. There is not much money on offer. Alexa pulls on tight leather jeans and a jazzy red top. Her face is painted and her black hair tied back. The acoustics are dreadful. She gives it her best shot. The boozy crowd is slow to respond until a big black guy comes up to the mike and starts to blow on a harmonica. Now they are clapping to the rhythm. He sings in a strong resonant voice. Mesmerised, Alexa finds herself joining in, harmonising. The big guy beckons her up to the stage. He starts a new number, a popular one which she has heard on a juke box. They seem to fit right away. Afterwards he tells her his name is Ludo, a short form of Ludovic. She wonders if her worries could be over.

*

Kate has been anxious for some time. The list of rural Post Offices proposed for closure includes the one contained within her small shop. Petitions have been signed and letters written to people of influence. They can only wait for officialdom to cast its vote.

Alicky wants another puppy. Kate shivers, she thinks about what happened with the last one. The boy had not known his own strength. Kate wonders about an older dog from the rescue centre. She hates to disappoint.

There is no work now for John Alec, a fall at the garage has damaged his back. Seòras Ruadh is sorry but the *bodach* should not have been near the pit. He offers a small sum of compensation. Kate is glad to accept. John Alec does not remember his mishap.

Ludo pushes shut the door with his foot. The place is a mess. Alexa is in her white bathrobe, her hair swings loose, her face looks vulnerable without make up. She is strumming on an old acoustic guitar nobody has bothered with for a long time. Alexa is humming gently as her fingers stroke the strings. He can tell that something is wrong. There is just room on the worktop for the sack of groceries. Ludo reaches out his arms, concerned and caring. She lets him hold her. It was this television programme, she says. Some Scottish guy, lean faced and long haired, singing about his homeland and how he wanted to go back. Caledonia is calling him and now he is going home. She hates herself for her weakness but the soulful melody has made her cry for the people and the past that she has discarded. Ludo tells her they have to talk. It is never too late.

In the lateness of the year Kate smells the presence of winter. Geese are on the move. The Post Office will remain, isolation is its saviour. Along with the Christmas mail a letter comes. She reads it many times over, afraid that there may have been a mistake. Hopes must not be raised. Perhaps she has not understood properly. A long-term partner is described. This is not a concern; they are in more tolerant times. A black man is soon to be President of the United States.

She watches John Alec walk slowly to the house with Rusty on a lead. The brown dog knows the way home. Alicky is on the settee strumming on his guitar, strumming and singing,

'My Bonnie flies over the Ocean, My Bonnie flies over the Sea'

Kate is not sure whether to smile or weep. It will not be his Bonnie. It will be the mother who abandoned him thirteen years ago coming home at last.

THE CONTRIBUTORS

Frances Abbot has lived in the Highlands for thirty-five years. Before becoming a member of Ross-shire Writers her writing was confined to plays written for and performed by children, community groups and arts organisations. Since joining the group she has concentrated on short stories. This publication is their first outing.

Sandra Bain is a native of the Black Isle but has worked in Perthshire and Peru. She has had non-fiction articles published and is Editor of the quarterly magazine of the Scottish Fellowship of Christian Writers. In 2005 her book on the history of Tore School was published.

Carol Fenelon is a published poet. She wrote professionally as part of her employment for many years and is a founder member of Ross-shire Writers.

Reg Holder grew up in East Africa, coming to the UK to train for the Merchant Navy. He is a Master Mariner and after sailing on cargo ships and tankers came ashore as a pilot, working in oil terminals. He is now a marine consultant and he and his wife Pat have lived in Ross-shire for the last eleven years.

Leonard A. Hollywood has been a member of Ross-shire Writers since its inception. He lives in Inverness.

Louise James has lived in Scotland since 2003, although she has spent countless days over the years in the islands and highlands on hillwalking adventures. She tries to 'grow where she is planted', drawing on her Canadian roots, as well as her twenty years in Yorkshire, to inspire her writing.

Fiona Lang is originally from Edinburgh. She studied drawing and painting at Duncan of Jordanstone College of Art, Dundee, and then retrained in biotechnology. She had been writing in secret for a number of years before a fortuitous chance meeting led to an invitation to join the Ross-shire Writers. This wonderful, highly varied and supportive group of people have enticed her out of the writing closet. These are her first published stories.

Christina Macdonald was born and brought up in Stornoway and has lived in Ross-shire for almost 30 years. She has been involved in writing in various genres all her adult life and has had articles and letters published in local newspapers. She had a Christmas story published in *The Ross-shire Journal*, a poem published in *The Stornoway Gazette* this year and in 2005 won first prize in an Age Concern (Scotland) short story competition.

June Munro has Highland roots and lives in the tropical end of the Struie. She has travelled widely and is a dedicated people watcher. Some of her pieces have been published in women's magazines.

Jim Piper lives near Strathpeffer. His writing tends to be humorous and one of his poems has been published in *The Ross-shire Journal*. He enjoys water colour painting and the outdoors – walking and gardening.

Henriette A.O. Stewart was born and grew up in Denmark, but has lived in Scotland for eighteen years. She started writing six years ago when she joined a creative writing class (later Ross-shire Writers). She is currently a full time student at Inverness College.
.

Catriona (MacRitchie) Tawse grew up in Achiltibuie, was educated at Dingwall Academy; then divided her time between west and east coast as a Primary Teacher and in a variety of other occupations. After returning to this area she became involved in short story writing with Ross-shire Writers. Her story, Wildsong, won first prize at the Northern Lights Festival in Durness in 2007 and she has had articles published. in Aberdeen. She enjoys travelling to concerts by her favourite band and spends time each summer learning Gaelic at Sabhal Mòr Ostaig in Skye